WHO
IS
THIS
JESUS?

WHO
IS
THIS
JESUS?

D. T. Niles

Nashville   **ABINGDON PRESS**   New York

To

Tracy and Edith Strong

PREFACE

This is a new book as well as an old one. It is new because I am seeking, for the first time in my writing, to deal directly with the christological question. That is not to say that this book is about Christology in any dogmatic sense. It is an attempt, rather, to describe four things: What does Jesus look like when we look at him? What does it feel like when he looks at us? What does it seem like when he is presented to others? What does he act like when we join company with him on the way?

It is natural, therefore, that this book should also turn out to be an old book, for these themes have occupied my work and my writing across the years. Thus, in discussing the significance of Christ in relation to other religions, I am reverting to issues dealt with toward the close of my book *Reading the Bible Today*, and in my book *The Preacher's Task and the Stone of Stumbling*. The chapter on "The Finality of Jesus Christ" is my contribution to a symposium edited by Dr. Dow Kirkpatrick and published by Abingdon Press in 1966, while the two chapters on "The Story the Gospels Tell" are largely a condensation of my book *Living with the Gospel. Reading the Bible Today* and *Living with*

7

the Gospel are both books in the "World Christian Books" series.

I am grateful to Abingdon Press for permission to include in this book the essay on "The Finality of Jesus Christ," for which they hold the copyright, and to Lutterworth Press and "World Christian Books" for permission to quote from *Reading the Bible Today* and to make the condensation of *Living with the Gospel,* for which they hold the copyright. With respect to the last, a further word of explanation is also necessary, for it is normally reprehensible when an author makes a new book out of an old one. The point is that in my little book *Living with the Gospel,* I was simply retelling the Gospel story; so that in seeking to tell it again, I found it normal to tell it again in the same way. Besides, only by the writing of this book now have I been able to fulfill my intention in writing the other book then. However, for the purpose of the "World Christian Books" series, the earlier book is still relevant as an aid to people in their reading of the Gospels.

It is not always possible to sit down and write a book. A book grows, and parts of it may get written, and perhaps also published, according to needs and opportunities which arise. All I can do is to ask pardon of reader and publisher for the way in which this book has taken shape and the ways in which it is dependent on my other writings.

It so happened that the Ayer lectures and the Haskel lectures followed each other, so that I was able to use the same lectures for both series. However, in preparing the lectures for publication, I had to make one big change. The last lecture of my series was in the form of a postscript under the title, "The Call to Remember." This lecture I have replaced in the book with a chapter on "The Mysteries of the Kingdom." I have done this because, both at Colgate-Rochester Divinity School where the Ayer lectures were delivered, and at the Graduate School of Theology, Oberlin, Ohio, where the Haskell lectures were delivered, the discussions which followed the lectures raised questions which I felt I had to deal with when the lectures were published. (The Ayer lectures were four in number and the Haskell lectures six. The two additional lectures in the Haskell series were the two on "The Story the Gospels Tell.")

It now only remains for me to thank the Ayer Lecture Foundation and the Haskell Lecture Foundation for their kindness in inviting me to give these series of lectures.

I have dedicated this book to Tracy and Edith Strong, in affectionate gratitude for many personal kindnesses both to me and to my wife. It was a privilege to work under Tracy Strong in my first appointment to an ecumenical post. He was General Secretary of the World Alliance of YMCAs when I worked on its staff in 1939-40. I owe to his influence, no less than to that of others, the conviction that, in the last analysis, "who Jesus is" is what must determine the work we do and the way in which we must do it.

D. T. NILES

CONTENTS

11

CHAPTER 1

There always arrives a time in the life of a writer or preacher when, as it were, he comes back to the central issues that have engaged his heart and mind across the years. The Ayer and Haskell lectures determined this time for me. My first book, published in 1938, bore the title *Sir, We Would See Jesus. Who Is This Jesus?* is the title of this book now.

What I have attempted is to state as simply as I can the message one hears as one listens to the biblical testimony to Jesus Christ; and then to set that testimony within the confusions and controversies of religious debate in their contemporary forms. It is my conviction that only as we listen to the biblical testimony to Jesus Christ in the actual language and idiom in which that testimony is given shall we be able to reinterpret that testimony for our own day and generation.

Too many, too often and too quickly, stop listening to what the records actually do say, because they will not undertake the discipline of learning the ways of speech and expression of those records. Hence they are not aware of what they lose, even though the loss be inevitable, when they transpose the testimony from one thought-form to another. Transposition and translation are indeed necessary to make the testimony contemporary, but it is always that which has been missed in the process which claims attention from the next generation of scholars and preachers.

WHO
IS
THIS
JESUS?

My wife was a teacher in a Christian girls' high school when I married her. Apart from teaching music and singing, she was also the guide captain in the school. In many ways the guide captain served also as a pastor, the person who dealt in a pastoral way with the girls' personal problems and needs. One of the most talented pupils in the school, a Hindu, was particularly close to my wife because she was a patrol leader in the guide company. She was also a good violinist and, though a Hindu, played the violin for the singing in the church. She was a very likeable and alive person. During a crisis in the girl's life, my wife prayed with her and for her and also found real opportunity to talk to her about Jesus Christ. About the time that the girl was to leave school, she was very close to the decision to become a Christian, but she did not. In the final conversation that she had with my wife on this subject, she said that she had pondered the whole question but could not persuade herself that it was worth giving up her own Hindu home and her immediate Hindu community in order to become a member of the Christian church. She had no intention of rejecting the claims of Jesus Christ on her own life, nor of pronouncing a judgment on the Christian community; but she felt that she could be true to him without adding to her decision all the burdens that would arise if she should choose to belong to the Christian community also. She said to my wife, "You will continue to love me still, but that is no reason why I should become a Christian."

Whenever I have thought about Jesus Christ and who he is, this particular incident has a way of intruding into my thinking. I myself was involved in this incident because I too prayed with this girl during the days of her decision. I have never been able to forget the fact that somehow Jesus was able to stand apart from the Christian community in the thinking and deciding of someone whom he had surely managed to find.

The Nature of the Question

I believe fully that a decision to follow Jesus Christ is inextricably linked with the decision to become a member of the Christian church. There is a very true sense in which the refusal to become a Christian constitutes also a refusal to belong to Christ. The story that I have related is not intended to question the theology of this connection between Jesus Christ and his church. It is related rather to show that, in spite of this connection, men and women do find themselves confronted by Jesus alone and, whatever their decision, it is on the distinctive question of who he is that that decision has turned.

Though in the story which I have related there was no intention to pronounce a judgment on the Christian community, sometimes the way in which the decision for or against Jesus Christ presents itself to a person makes a judgment on the Christian community also inevitable. After our marriage, my wife and I lived in the village where the school is at which my wife taught. A member of that village community met us one day and told us that he was being faced with the decision to become a Christian. He belonged to one of what we call the depressed class groups. "We are told," he said, "that if we become Christians, we can have the help of the church and of the missionaries to provide for us economic and educational uplift." But, as he put it, his problem was that he could not bring himself to practice the dishonesties that were necessary if he were to find favor with the missionaries and with those in authority in the church. He decided to remain as he was.

This incident revealed to me something about the nature of the Christian church which I had not seen before. The Hindu community has no religious organization, nor has the Buddhist. They have religious institutions, but there is no organization that dispenses patronage and in which careerism is both a temptation and a necessity. The very nature of the church's task in the world has made the church a socio-religious organization. To have such an organization linked theologically to Jesus Christ produces a number of problems which are well-nigh insoluble. The Gospel records show how Jesus Christ came into conflict with the socio-religious organization of his own time and people. The crux of the matter lies in recognizing that such a conflict is not only inevitable, but also legitimate. The crucifixion was not a disaster which overtook Jesus. It was the only possible outcome of that conflict in which Jesus was involved: an outcome which is the source of the illumination, power, and authority which men have needed to give their own answers to this conflict, as they have faced it in every generation and in every varying situation. The particular person I have been talking about found himself unable to face the question, "Who is this Jesus?" by itself. He could not get it disentangled from a host of other questions in which it was enmeshed. All the more reason, then, that we look alone at the question of Jesus Christ. Who is he?

There is a third person I want to talk about. He is a personal friend of mine who is also our family doctor. He too is a Hindu. The apostle Paul speaks of the fruit of the Spirit as love, joy, peace, patience, kindness, goodness, faithfulness, gentleness, self-control (Gal. 5:22). By using the singular, the "fruit of the Spirit," Paul is not merely talking of these various virtues and qualities, but about the way in which they belong together and interpenetrate one another. (When he speaks of the works of the flesh, he talks in the plural.) Speaking quite deliberately, I would say that one of the best examples I know of the fruit of the Spirit, as Paul has defined it, is this doctor friend of mine. I am quite aware that we have a tendency to look at our fellow Christians under a microscope, whereas we look at other good men through a telescope. And yet I am prepared to stand by my statement. My object in making it, however, is not to state a comparison between Hindu and Christian, but to point to the fact itself that here in a Hindu is the fruit of the Spirit.

But why do I speak of a Hindu in Christian terms? Only because I cannot find in Hinduism itself a satisfying explanation of the source and vitality of true goodness. Only in Jesus Christ and the forgiveness wrought by him, and only in the Holy Spirit and the energy he bestows do I discern an adequate explanation of how man can be good.

Here we see from another angle the point of the question: Who is this Jesus? What is his relation to men, to all men, to each man? To think of Jesus as the founder of a religion and, therefore, to seek an answer to the question, "Who is Jesus?" by approaching it from within that religion seems to me to be quite misleading. The question, "Who is Jesus?" cannot be an important question unless it is also a question concerning every man.

Let what I have said so far serve to provide a glimpse into the kind of questioning I find myself grappling with as I seek to understand the true meaning of who Jesus is and the implications thereof. The particular twists and turns of the argument may otherwise be quite puzzling. Each man comes to the question, "Who is this Jesus?" by his own particular road. No one can avoid the junction where these roads meet, but the road by which each has arrived at the junction has it own interpretative significance. As I face the question, therefore, I shall want to know how it is that this question is thrust on us at all, how this question disentangles itself from all connected questions while at the same time bearing the burden of them, and also how it happens that this question becomes a question concerning every man.

The Force of the Testimony

Our first task will be to look at the nature of the testimony of the Gospel records, and then to listen to the story of Jesus as the Gospels actually tell it. I have decided to do this because, again and again, when participating in discussions on this subject or reading about it in books, I have been struck by the way in which the argument often tended to skirt the story of Jesus itself. I am convinced that there is no substitute for listening to the whole story without fragmentation, and of the actual impact of that story when it is heard as a whole.

The fact of Jesus was never simply a fact recorded but, from the beginning, was a fact proclaimed. The necessity for and the legitimacy of the proclamation rested on the resurrection event. When, in the Gospel narrative, the risen Christ asked those early witnesses to "go and tell," he was asking them to bear testimony to something that had happened to him, and not simply to something that had happened to them. If not for the resurrection, it would have been the teachings of Jesus that his disciples taught, while the incidents of his life would have been related as demonstrating the import of those teachings. The situation in the New Testament, however, is that Jesus himself is the one who is proclaimed, while the incidents in his life are seen as pointers to his true identity. His teachings become significant because it was he who taught them. "It was said to the men of old, . . . but I say to you" (Matt. 5:21) is a formula that points to him and to his credentials. The Fourth Evangelist says plainly, "The law was given through Moses; grace and truth came through Jesus Christ" (John 1:17). In Matthew's Gospel, the Sermon on the Mount takes the place of the commandments and teachings that Moses brought down from Mount Sinai. Matthew makes clear that what is here set forth is not an alternative law, but an announcement of the blessedness that will accrue because the kingdom of God had come, and of the consequences and implications of that blessedness for daily living. Thus when it is said, "Blessed are the poor," what is affirmed is not the blessedness of poverty but the blessedness that the poor will experience because God's kingdom has come. Or when it is said, "You are the light of the world," what is affirmed is not merely the obligation to be the light that belongs to the children of the kingdom, but the promise that he who ushers in the kingdom will set aflame the lives of those who accept it. The accent every time is on Jesus himself. It is he who is proclaimed.

In many discussions today on the nature and method of Christian witness, there is being emphasized what has come to be called the "Christian presence." This is right. But within this phrase there is sometimes hidden the idea that the business of the Christian is to repeat Jesus Christ. This cannot be done. The Christian's business is to point away from himself to Jesus Christ. The presence of the Christian in any situation must be such that it makes clamant the question,

Who Is This Jesus?

"Who is this Jesus Christ that this man serves as Lord?" What the Gospels do is to show what the presence of Jesus Christ meant to those among whom he lived and what, therefore, happened both to them and to him. The Christian presence must mean that these things are happening again and that, therefore, Christ himself is present, asking to be identified and acknowledged.

In Mark's Gospel

The point of departure of Mark's Gospel is Peter. After fifteen verses of introduction, the Gospel begins with the call of Peter and goes on to describe in some detail that first memorable day which Peter spent with his Lord. Jesus had come to him, walking along the shores of the Sea of Galilee, the shores he knew so well; found him at his normal occupation; and drew him into a discipleship that overturned his world and shattered him, and made both anew. Jesus had said, "Follow me, and I will make you become a fisher of men." Those words had divided Peter's life in two.

The consequence of Jesus for each man and for all men is what Mark's Gospel is about. The axis on which it turns is *man and the Son of man who was the Son of God.* Mark's method is to show that the ministry of Jesus Christ is a ministry with consequences for every man, because its true intention is to engage in conflict and overthrow the powers of evil by which all men are enslaved and enfeebled. The stronger has come to despoil the house of the strong (Mark 3:27). After narrating the call of Simon Peter, the Gospel piles five miracles one on top of the other. In the synagogue at Caper-

naum, Jesus is confronted by a man in the grip of the power
of evil. He knows who Jesus is but is quite unable to belong
to him. Jesus sets him free to belong. Jesus goes from the
synagogue to the house of Simon Peter. The lady of the
house, Simon's mother-in-law, is unable to welcome him or
offer him hospitality. She is ill. Jesus takes her by the hand
and lifts her up, and the fever leaves her, so that she is then
able to serve them. The next day, on the road, a leper meets
him. He is an outcast from human society. He is unclean.
But he knows that Jesus can cleanse him. Jesus stretches out
his hand and touches him. That touch transforms his whole
life. By it he is restored to human fellowship. Again at Capernaum, some days afterward, Jesus is preaching. A paralytic is
brought to him. This man arrives borne on the faith of others.
But he himself is quite helpless. His physical condition, however, is simply part of his total condition. Conscious sin has
broken his relationship with God. Jesus does what God alone
can do—he pronounces his sins forgiven. The man goes
home a witness to the glory of God. The fifth in the series of
miracles is the healing of the man with the withered hand.
From the way the story is told, it looks as if the man had
been brought there to find out what Jesus would do. Would
Jesus uphold the law of the Sabbath or would he heal the
man? The story says quite plainly that Jesus was angry and
sad. Why use the institutions of religion to bind men with
fetters? When Jesus said to the man with the withered hand,
"Stretch it out," God himself was declared free from those
institutions of religion by which men sought to channel his
goodness and regulate his power.

"Man and the Son of man"—that, we said, was the axis

on which Mark's Gospel turns. The fulcrum of this axis is right in the center of the Gospel, for Mark puts into the very middle of the story of Jesus the question which Jesus asked his disciples: "Who do you say that I am?" (Mark 8:29). Peter answers him, "You are the Christ." Immediately follow the words of Jesus, teaching them that the "Son of man must suffer many things, and be rejected by the custodians of religion and those in authority, and be killed, and after three days rise again." Mark adds the words, "And he said this plainly" (see Mark 8:31-32). By the affirmation that he is the Christ, there is affirmed that he is God's deed of deliverance of his people. By the affirmation that he must suffer and be rejected and be killed, there is affirmed that in him Israel's mission as servant will be fulfilled. By the affirmation that he is the Son of man, there is affirmed that by him the "new age" for all men will be inaugurated. In the double title— Son of man and Son of God—lies the burden of this Gospel's testimony. How distorted that testimony becomes when the reference to God is declared to be out of court and Jesus is simply explained as man among men or even as man for others! Jesus is man, in whom and by whom men become men, precisely because in him God wrought for man an ending and a new beginning.

The Gospel of Mark opens with the words, "The beginning of the gospel of Jesus Christ, the Son of God." It is the beginning of a story that Mark is about to record. When the Christ came, so every Jew believed, he would set his people free. Peter had seen that this ministry of the Christ was not simply for Israel but for all men and women. What was more, it was a ministry without an ending. Peter saw how he himself was going to be a part of that ongoing ministry. He also saw how there would be others to follow him. It may be that, as scholars say, the ending of Mark's Gospel is lost. But I like to think of it as a Gospel which tells the story of a beginning, but leaves the telling of that story in the middle of a sentence. We too in our day and generation, as generations before us and generations after us, must live with him and, living with him, make up our minds as to who he is.

In Matthew's Gospel

The testimony of Matthew's Gospel is conditioned by the first problem which the witnesses to Jesus faced in their time and in their situation. They were Jews proclaiming that the Messiah had come. The expectation of the Messiah was an integral part of the Jewish faith. But, whereas that faith was so taught and practiced that it looked forward to the coming of the Messiah, hardly any thought or preparation had gone into the question of what would happen to this faith and its practices when the Messiah actually came. The result of this lack of preparation was a complete unreadiness to receive the Messiah when he did come. The testimony of Matthew's Gospel is a testimony of those who received him and, therefore, is concerned with their confession of him before their fellows who suspected them of disloyalty. They found that they had to answer the question, "Who is Jesus?" and defend their answer in terms of the religious history of the race. Jesus Christ could not be a completely discontinuous event. Thus *Israel, the New Israel, and the Christ* is the axis on which Matthew's Gospel turns.

The Gospel begins with the declaration that Jesus Christ is the son of David, the son of Abraham. Matthew alone, of the first three evangelists, stresses the fact that the immediate ministry of Jesus was to the lost house of Israel (Matt. 10:6; 15:24). The point the Gospel makes is not that Jesus was interested in Israel alone, but that unless his ministry is seen as a ministry to Israel, it is not possible to see the true significance of that ministry. The call to Abraham was that in him all the nations of the world should find their blessing (Gen. 12:2). It is this call which Jesus is set forth as fulfilling. In the great commission with which the Gospel ends, the nations are clearly in view. "I shall bless you and in you the nations shall be blessed" was the promise given to Abraham; and it is this precise promise that is the burden of the great commission: "Go and disciple the nations" (see Matt. 28:19).

Jesus was the son of David because it was David's kingdom that came to its fulfillment in Jesus. The kingdom of David, in Jewish thought and expectation, did not simply point to the golden age of Israel which some day would be restored; it pointed rather to the mission of Israel and to that kingdom into which the nations would be gathered. "At that time Jerusalem shall be called the throne of the Lord, and all the nations shall gather to it." (Jer. 3:17.) During one of the discussions which Jesus had with the Pharisees, he asked them this question: "If the Christ is the son of David, how is it that David calls him Lord?" (see Matt. 22:41-43). In this question, Jesus is quoting from Psalm 110, in which the Anointed of God is described as a "priest for ever after the order of Melchizedek." Melchizedek was he to whom Abraham made his offering of thanksgiving after victory (Gen.

14:20). Here is Jesus' thought of himself as the fulfillment of that purpose of God which reaches out beyond the limits of the people of Israel, the children of Abraham.

The conviction in the mind of Jesus that he was the fulfillment of the destiny of Israel finds expression in the baptism story. His ministry begins with the assurance that he is God's beloved Son (Matt. 3:17), bringing together the description both of Israel as Son (Psalm 2:7) and as beloved servant (Isa. 42:1). Indeed, there is little doubt that it is to Jesus himself that the First Evangelist owes the parallelism which he works out between the life of Jesus and the history of Israel. Let us look at just two examples: the first, a parallel which the evangelist himself points out; and the second, a parallel which Jesus deliberately occasions. Herod, in trying to kill the child Jesus, had slain the children in Bethlehem. This had made necessary the flight of the holy family to Egypt (Matt. 2:13-18). The evangelist interprets this story as a repetition of an earlier event in the story of Israel. The ten tribes were lost in exile and mourned for, but, as Jeremiah had promised, Judah had come back from the land of the enemy (Jer. 31:15-16). This return from Babylon was, in its turn, a repetition of that act by which God brought Israel from the bondage of Egypt. So that in quoting Hosea, "Out of Egypt I called my son" (Hos. 11:1), and in linking it with the other quotation from Jeremiah, Matthew makes it explicit that it is Jesus the Son whom the sonship of Israel prefigured.

The parallel with the Old Testament story which Jesus occasioned is found during the events of his last week in Jerusalem. He crowded into this week many actions, each of which was an allusion to an earlier word or event to be found in the Old Testament. He came into Jerusalem riding on an ass, pointing a parallel to Zechariah 9:9. He came accompanied by the cry "Hosanna," suggesting an echo of Psalm 118:26. He showed his zeal to cleanse the temple, fulfilling Jeremiah 7:11. He cursed the fig tree with leaves but without fruit, recalling Jeremiah 8:13. Isaac was the son of promise to Abraham; Jesus was the son of promise to Mary. Israel was delivered from the hand of Pharaoh and brought out of Egypt; Jesus was delivered from the hand of Herod and brought out of Egypt. Israel passed through the Red Sea; Jesus passed through the waters of baptism at the river Jordan. Israel was alone with God in the wilderness for forty years; Jesus was alone with God in the wilderness for forty days. Israel's history as a kingdom was one of hopeful beginnings which finally ended in tragedy; the ministry of Jesus also was one of hopeful beginnings which ended on a cross. Israel came back from exile; Jesus rose from the dead. The Old Testament story is indeed the story of the Son, but whereas disobedience characterized Israel's history, Jesus was the perfectly obedient one. Obedience is true fulfillment. The Scriptures were fulfilled in him because he obeyed.

It is from this vantage point of the obedience of Jesus Christ that the Gospel bears testimony also to the way in which he fulfilled Israel's law, replaced Israel's temple, and satisfied Israel's hope. The news announced is that the Sabbath law is broken, that the temple veil is rent, and that the King of the Jews hangs on a cross.

This fulfillment of the old in the new, nevertheless, is not at all an obvious truth. To the Jews, who still live by the Old Testament, this is even today no truth at all. Did not

Saul of Tarsus deny this fulfillment, with every energy of his mind and all the strength of persecuting zeal, until he met Jesus? Indeed, Jesus is recognized as "he who fulfills" only by those who have met him and who, in that meeting, have been challenged by his presence. The testimony of the First Evangelist, about the way in which Jesus Christ was the fulfillment of the old covenant, rests for its proof ultimately on what Jesus himself did when men encountered him. In consequence, merely to think of events in the New Testament as fulfilling texts in the Old Testament is to reduce a living experience into a theorem in geometry. Only successful evangelism can furnish the proof that Jesus is the fulfillment of prophecy. We must lead men into a meeting with him.

The question, "Who is the Christ?" lies embedded in every religion and every man's religious history. The ways in which that question becomes separated from that history are various, but the question itself does become for every man, every religious man, the question which he must answer. The burden of the testimony of the First Evangelist is to explain how this question became central to the people among whom Jesus lived, and to those in the surrounding religious world. He helps us to grasp the inwardness of the sense of judgment which men felt when they met with Jesus; and the way in which, both to those who accepted him and to those who rejected him, he became contemporary. How significant it is, that this Gospel which opens its record of the public ministry of Jesus with the Beatitudes closes that record with his parable of the great judgment in which blessedness is the portion of those who simply have served him in his anonymity! The question, "Who is Jesus Christ?" is here firmly taken out of

27

the realm of religious debate and set squarely in the world of human relationships.

In Luke's Gospel

Luke's Gospel has its face set toward Rome. It is the declaration of the faith which Paul had proclaimed, and for which he was to be tried by Caesar. The axis on which this Gospel turns is the *nations and the reign of God*. The kingdom of God has come. Jesus has broken down every wall of partition. Men are reconciled to one another and to God. The nations are called to repentance.

There are two special emphases in Luke's Gospel. The first is that what he is going to write about is an event which belongs to the course of secular events. The story is dated in the fifteenth year of the reign of Tiberius Caesar, Pontius Pilate being governor of Judea and Herod being tetrarch of Galilee, in the high priesthood of Annas and Caiaphas (Luke 3:1-2). The happenings which Luke is going to talk about are datable. His second emphasis is on the unfinished nature of the story he is telling. He opens his Gospel with a reference to the "things which have been accomplished among us," thus suggesting that something has happened, something has been accomplished, with which men must reckon hereafter. Also, in the Acts of the Apostles, he refers to his Gospel as a book concerning "all that Jesus began to do and teach" (Acts 1:1). He intends the Acts of the Apostles as a continuation and consequence of that beginning.

But what was it that was begun? The answer is provided by the opening story of the ministry of Jesus, the story of his sermon at Nazareth. "The Spirit of the Lord is upon me, because he has anointed me to preach good news to the poor. He has sent me to proclaim release to the captives and recovering of sight to the blind, to set at liberty those who are oppressed, to proclaim the acceptable year of the Lord." (Luke 4:18-19.) These are secular happenings. Indeed, when Luke talks about the reign of God, he uses that word "reign" not in any specifically religious sense. He says quite simply and directly: God is the king of this world and its people, and this king is active on behalf of them all.

The witness in Mark's Gospel is a particular man, Peter. The witness in Matthew's Gospel is the Jewish-Christian community. The witness in Luke's Gospel is a human company: men and women, Jews and Gentiles, bond and free, who have come together around Jesus Christ, and belong together as those who belong to him.

In the sermon at Nazareth, with which the Gospel begins its narrative of the ministry of Jesus, the emphasis is already made on the inclusiveness of God's reign and God's grace. "There were many widows in Israel in the days of Elijah, . . ." says Jesus, "and Elijah was sent to none of them but only to Zarephath, in the land of Sidon, to a woman who was a widow. And there were many lepers in Israel in the time of the prophet Elisha; and none of them was cleansed but only Naaman the Syrian" (Luke 4:25-27). In many other ways too, all peculiar to Luke, can be discerned this particular quality of his testimony. He underlines the fact that, when the Samaritans would not receive Jesus because he was on his way to Jerusalem, and James and John wanted to bring down fire and consume them, Jesus rebuked them and simply went on to another village. He follows immediately with the story of the mission of the seventy—a mission not confined to Israel but extending to every town and place where Jesus himself was about to come (Luke 9:51–10:1). Also, it is in this third Gospel only that we have our Lord's parable of the good Samaritan (Luke 10:30-35). Further, there is the significant feature in Luke's arrangement of events, whereby the story he puts at the gateway to Judea is the cure of ten lepers of whom only a Samaritan came back to give thanks (Luke 17:11-19). And then, there is the fact worth noting that Luke alone tells us of the prayer of Jesus uttered as the Roman soldiers crucified him: "Father, forgive them; for they know not what they do" (Luke 23:34).

It is the whole world which is in view in this third Gospel. The atmosphere is that of a journey, and the story is pressed to the far horizons. Appropriately, the third Gospel ends with the words, "Thus it is written, that the Christ should suffer and the third day rise from the dead, and that repentance and forgiveness of sins should be preached in his name to all nations, beginning from Jerusalem" (Luke 24:46-47).

We may summarize what Luke's answer is to the question, "Who is this Jesus?" by saying that Jesus is he in whom the life of the world finds its wholeness. The oppressed are delivered, the mighty are brought low, Jew and Gentile are reconciled, the Samaritan comes to give God thanks, for all men the prayer of forgiveness has been prayed. God's reign has become active in Jesus Christ and is on the march along the highways of the world to every corner of God's earth. Reading three of the parables which are peculiar to the Third Evangelist, I have often been struck by the possibility in them of a reference to this theme. In the parable of the rich man and Lazarus, the dogs too find a place, for they come and lick the poor man's sores. The Jews referred to the Gentiles as dogs; but whereas the dogs did for the poor man what was in their power to do, from the table of the rich Jew not even the crumbs were available (Luke 16:19-20). In the parable of the prodigal son, could it be that the Gentiles were the son who was prodigal in the far country, while the Jews were the elder son who, even though he remained in the father's house, was still estranged from his father's love? But the father's home was for Jew and Gentile alike (Luke 15:11-12). In the parable of the woman who lost one coin out of the ten on her head-chain, the point is well made that the whole chain would be useless till that one coin is found and restored to its place in the chain (Luke 15:8-9). The Lucan testimony to the significance of Jesus is that in him and because of him men find one another. All the distinctions of class, race, age, and sex are wiped out. Salvation has come to all nations; that is, to every particularity in which men live and by which their community is defined. No wonder this Gospel traces the genealogy of Jesus back to Adam, and makes the point that, when Jesus was born, a census was being taken so that God himself was counted among men.

In John's Gospel

In the fourth Gospel, the evangelist manages to make Jesus his own witness. The axis on which this Gospel turns is the *world and the Word*. John's thought is in cosmic dimensions. To the question, "Who is this Jesus?" the synoptists suggest answers in terms of what it means for men that Jesus happened. Because of Jesus men find themselves, they find God, and they find one another. In the fourth Gospel, the answer provided is in the passive voice. Men come to the experience of being found, of being accepted. They experience deliverance from the disharmonies of nature and the chaos in which human life is involved. The cosmos again becomes luminous with meaning. Men find themselves part of an ordered world. They experience what it means to belong to a world God created, which God loved, and which God redeemed.

The way in which this answer is provided by the Fourth Evangelist is to set Jesus Christ at the center of everything, so that everything arrives at its harmony in him. The Gospel relates seven miracles which Jesus did and calls them signs. They are the signs of God's presence and power in the midst of life. The first sign is at a wedding feast where he turns water into wine. In this story, three themes are woven together. Just as the drama of redemption will end with the marriage feast of the Lamb, so it begins at a marriage feast. At the first marriage, Jesus is a guest. At the second, he will be the bridegroom. The water which is turned into wine is water kept for the Jewish rites of purification. As Christ's ministry develops, not only are these rites of purification left behind, but for them is substituted the covenant of baptism. Not only so, but baptism itself leads into a new life where communion is established with God through Jesus—through his life that was given, through the wine that was spilled. So does the presence of Jesus make the difference at this wedding. The guest becomes the host. It is his wine that is served (John 2:1-11).

The second sign which is recorded is that of the healing of the son of an official in Capernaum. In this sign, a word that was spoken healed the boy, even though Jesus himself was far away (John 4:46-54). The third sign is a healing that took place on the Sabbath day. A man had been ill for thirty-eight years. He could have remained ill for one day longer. That was the burden of the protest of the Jews. But Jesus healed him and told him to carry his pallet home. The justification which Jesus gave for what he did was, "My Father is working still, and I am working" (John 5:2-18). Both these signs make the point that there is no restriction either of time or place to the working of God.

The fourth sign is set within the context of the Passover season. The sign itself was the provision of food. In the discourse that follows, Jesus says to the Jews, "I am the bread of life." Manna was provided by God to sustain the journey through the wilderness. Jesus is God's provision to sustain the journey of life. The presence of Jesus, with those on this journey, and under all circumstances, is further emphasized by the immediate sign which followed, the fifth in the series, when, in the middle of a storm at sea and in the dark, Jesus came to them walking on the water (John 6:16-21). It is generally accepted that the discourse in the fourth Gospel on the "bread of life" is a discourse on the meaning of the institution of Holy Communion. In the story of the garden of Eden, when man decides to be himself the arbiter of his own destiny, the one who will himself decide what is good and what is evil, God allows to man this responsibility and tells him that he will eat bread by the sweat of his brow (Gen. 3:17-18). Now it is this very bread, the result of man's toil and labor, which becomes the sign of God's presence with and providence for man. In the same story, the result of eating the forbidden fruit, of man deciding that he himself will choose what is allowed and what is forbidden, is that his eyes were opened. Whereas he was created to walk by faith, he has now made it necessary for himself to walk by sight. And yet the truth is that man walking by sight is still blind. He is born blind.

The sixth sign in the Gospel is the healing of the man born blind (John 9:1-12). He who is healed does not know who has healed him until he meets Jesus again. "No one has ever seen God; the only Son, who is in the bosom of the Father, he has made him known." (John 1:18.)

The seventh and last of the signs is the raising of Lazarus from the dead. It is the sign of final victory. Life is crowned with eternal life. The new creation reaches its fulfillment. The signature of death which man's sin occasioned is now erased (John 11:1-44).

In the Gospel, these seven signs go hand in hand with seven declarations which our Lord makes of himself. The formula which is used is the name of God as it was revealed to Moses: "I am" (Exod. 3:14). Right at the very beginning of the story, the Jews ask John the Baptist, "Who are you?" His answer is, "I am not." That is the verdict on that which is about to pass away. When the first disciples asked Jesus, "Where are you staying?" he said to them, "Come and see." They went and saw, and what they saw was the Father, because it was with him that Jesus stayed. So follow the great "I am" sayings: I am the bread of life; I am the light of the world; I am the door of the sheep; I am the good shepherd;

I am the resurrection and the life; I am the way, the truth, and the life; I am the true vine. By this "I am," life and its purposes, its possibilities and its privileges are reconstituted. Jesus becomes the way to live, the truth to live by, and the life itself. (See John 6:35; 8:12; 10:7; 10:11; 11:25; 14:6; 15:1.) Thus is fulfilled the purpose for which the Word became flesh. So the Gospel brings the story to a close with words which occur in it only: "It is finished"—the work of the Christ is over.

And yet it is not over, for there is still one more sign to record (John 21:4-14). The risen Christ stands on the shore of the Sea of Galilee where the disciples have gone fishing. It is the same old situation again. The circumstances of the common life have not changed. But the Christ is there, a presence on which his disciples can always depend, ready with his command to them as they fish, ready with his provision for them as they come ashore. In the invitation, "Come and dine," is the expression of the everlasting mercy.

Who then is this Jesus so proclaimed? Let the question wait until we rehearse the whole story of what happened— the story the Gospels tell.

CHAPTER 2

As we have seen, each Gospel adopts its own method of arranging the material and presenting the developing story. Especially in dealing with the teachings of Jesus, there is the obvious attempt of the synoptists to group together teachings on the same theme, while the Fourth Evangelist weaves into one continuous narrative, often in the form of a discussion, his own meditations on the teachings of Jesus with the teachings themselves.

Can the four records, then, be so harmonized as to be presented as one continuous story? I believe that they can, because the main chronology is clear, and the material for each part of the ministry of Jesus is fairly identifiable in the records. The synoptists give the details of the Galilean ministry, the Perean ministry is reported by Luke only, the Judean ministry is treated extensively by John, while both Luke and John tell the stories of the contact of Jesus with the Samaritans and of his visits to Samaria. Also, while the evangelists have attempted to group similar teaching material, they are aware of how his teachings developed with the developing situation, so that they do not take the grouping process so far as to obliterate traces of this development.

Since, then, it is within a natural discernible chronology that the drama of the Gospels is set, the possibility exists of dramatizing the story as a whole, as well as of so presenting it as to testify both to what happened and to its meaning.

WHAT
HAPPENED?
THE STORY
THE GOSPELS TELL (I)

The intention of the Gospel writers is neither to write a chronicle nor to compose a biography. What they do is to present a drama. Besides, the drama is so composed that to listen to it is to be drawn into it. Indeed, the Gospel writers make plain that the meaning of the story of Jesus is the meaning of our story also. When Jesus was crucified, his cross bore the inscription, "Jesus of Nazareth, King of the Jews." Those who fashioned the inscription meant it as an accusation, but Jesus made it his title. So it always is. The meaning of our lives is the meaning he assigns to them. We crucify him, and then accept that it was for us that he was crucified.

Who Is This Jesus?

The Drama Opens—The Perspective Set

The Gospel drama opens with a prologue in which three affirmations are made. First, Jesus is the deed of God. The birth stories of Matthew and Luke, as well as the opening paragraphs of John, make it clear that it is God whose actions the Gospels celebrate: "God so loved"; "God was in Christ"; "God commends his love." What God did was to live a human life, live it victoriously, and make it contemporary, so that men could participate in that life and, participating in it, find their fellowship with him.

This action of God, however, was not something entirely new. As the second affirmation of the Gospel prologue has it, the deed of God in Jesus was continuous with the drama of Israel. God had always, and from the beginning, been concerned with man. Man had always, and from the beginning, been under the pressure of God's advancing reign. Now, in Jesus, that which had been a blockade became an invasion. Of this continuity of God's action, Israel was both instrument and witness.

So follows the third affirmation of the Gospel prologue, that what had happened in Jesus was the end event. The first words of Mark's Gospel are, "The beginning of the gospel of Jesus Christ, the Son of God." A beginning of what? God's dwelling place was now with men. He had become Emmanuel—God with us. It was also the beginning of the final conflict between God and evil, of which Herod's attempt to kill the Christ child was no more than the first sign. And, in the third place, it was the beginning of the gathering together of the whole family of God, of which the gathering at Bethlehem was the first promise. Round the Christ child were gathered Jew and Gentile, the wise and the unlearned, the rich and poor, men and beasts, earth and heaven. It was the beginning of the end.

The Hidden Years—His Growing Thoughts

We pass from the beginning of the story of Jesus to an account of his public ministry. But in passing, pause to look at him during those thirty hidden years of which the Gospels tell us so little. There is only one incident in the Gospel story which belongs to this period, but it is one which sheds a great deal of light upon the growing thoughts of Jesus during this time.

He is twelve years of age; he has completed his formal education in the village synagogue school and, according to the usual custom, is taken to Jerusalem to be received along with the other boys of the same age as a "son of the Law," a grown-up member of the Jewish congregation. What impression did that first journey to Jerusalem make on the boy Jesus? There would be the exaltation of spirit resulting from the singing of the Psalms as the caravans moved on to the city of the great King and from the shout of joy that would go up as Jerusalem was sighted. There must have been also long and painful thoughts along the way, as pilgrims passed the crosses planted along the roadside on which those men had hung who only eighteen months earlier had partaken in a revolt against Rome under the leadership of a man called

Judas. As for the impression which the city itself and the temple made on Jesus, we can only guess what his thoughts were as he listened to the teaching of the rabbis when he was taken before them, and as he watched for the first time the goings-on in the temple market.

But even in this early incident in the life of Jesus can be seen the beginnings of that consuming sorrow for his people which later made him weep over Jerusalem saying, "Would that even today you knew the things that make for peace!" (Luke 19:42); that inner certainty which made him teach "as one who had authority, and not as the scribes" (Mark 1:22); and that holy indignation which burst forth when he drove out from the temple them that bought and sold (John 2:13-22). In John's Gospel the clearing of the temple market is the first incident in the ministry of Jesus. It is as though some fire had been smoldering in his soul for a long time and broke out in scorching flame at the first opportunity. "My Father's house," he cries out, "shall be called a house of prayer for all the nations. But you have made it a house of trade and a den of robbers" (see John 2:16; Mark 11:17). "My Father's house"—there is the announcement of who he is; "for all the nations"—there is the declaration of whom he is for; "but you"—there is the challenge flung out. "You have turned the court of the Gentiles in the temple into a market. You have made religion a means of worldly gain. You have arranged that man shall be exploited in the name of the service of God." Man—that was the central point of all of Jesus' concern. Man and all men—it was to them that his whole life was committed. He had come that not one man should be lost, but that all men should be saved and come to the knowledge of the truth (I Tim. 2:4).

The Beginning—Call and Commission

But how was this to be done? The Gospels tell us that Jesus wrestled with this question for forty days in the wilderness before he began his public ministry.

At the age of thirty he left his home in Nazareth and came down to Judea to receive, at the hands of John the Baptist, the baptism of repentance for the remission of sins. He who had no sin took his place among sinners. It was right in the eyes of God that this should be so. In answer to this obedience, when he was baptized, God said to him, "Thou art my beloved Son" (Mark 1:11). That was his mission and commission—"to be God's Son amidst the perplexities of daily life." The prophets of the Old Testament received from God a message to be delivered; their task was to speak. The calling of Jesus was to be—to be the Son of God living among men. In the case of the prophets, their message was greater than they; in the case of Jesus, he himself was the message.

But what did it mean to be the Son? What did it mean for him, what did it mean for others? Could being the Son mean comfort and a comfortable life? Bread, and with bread everything that is necessary for the life of the body? No, for man shall not live by bread alone. Bread is given to make it possible to live the life of sonship. It is given for the journey which God has commanded. Manna is for the pilgrimage. No, sonship can never be a means to comfortable living, for man is more than body and life is more than comfort.

41

Could sonship then mean a life specially protected by miracle and sustained by excitement, a life of waving flags and shouting slogans? No; for we tempt God's goodness when we first get thoroughly worked up about some cause, and then expect God to be on our side. The kingdom of God is like a lump of leaven which a woman hid in three measures of meal. It does not come with observation. Sonship implies no special claim on the power of God, and the pilgrim must be prepared for the routine drudgery of his daily march. Man is more than mind, and life is more than adventure.

Could it be possible then that sonship for man would mean the exercise of power and the road to it? Could this be the way that man, as spirit, would fulfill himself? No, for only to God may men bend the knee; whereas the only way to power as power was to bend the knee to it, to make it the goal, one's all-absorbing quest. Besides, power to order the lives of our fellows never provides us with the means of winning their allegiance to God. Men can only be loved into God's kingdom, they cannot be organized into it. The pilgrim must reach the promised land on his own feet.

No wonder the way of Jesus with men cuts across all human ways! There are those who promise bread; Jesus promises the Word of God. There are those who promise processions and crusading enthusiasms; Jesus promises the quietness of faith. There are those who promise an ordered life and the maintenance of human rights; Jesus promises the maintenance of God's sovereignty. The frontier of decision to which Jesus pushes every man is a frontier created by God's promises and by his demands; no human cause is identical with God's cause.

Jesus and Men—Challenge and Opposition

It is best at this point to consider, side by side with the decisions of Jesus about man, the actual groups of men whom the Gospels mention as having in one way or another come into conflict with Jesus; and ultimately together as having contrived his death. A brief study of these groups will help us to understand the way in which the decisions which Jesus made in the wilderness affected the men among whom he lived and to whom he took his message.

Six groups are identified in the Gospel narrative: the Romans, the Sadducees, the scribes, the Pharisees, the Herodians, and the Zealots.

The Romans were the guardians of law and order. They had established peace and orderly government in the then-known world. Jesus thrust on them a choice between truth and policy, between doing right and maintaining peace. Pilate, preferring policy to truth, washed his hands and delivered Jesus to be crucified.

The Sadducees were the guardians of worship. It was their responsibility to maintain the temple and the observance of the temple ritual. When Jesus said, "Destroy this temple" (John 2:19), he was challenging the very reason for which the Sadducees existed. Moreover, the Sadducees were the local group which wielded power under the Romans. They represented whatever measure of self-government the Jews possessed. When Caiaphas said, "It is better that one man should die rather than that the whole nation should perish" (see John 11:50), he was putting into words the bitter choice which Jesus was forcing them to make. Jesus was revolutionary both in religion and in politics; while the Sadducees were committed to, indeed were responsible for, preserving things as they were. They decided to preserve themselves at the cost of handing Jesus over to the Romans to be killed.

The scribes were the guardians of orthodoxy. They had been engaged for generations in building up the "tradition" which constituted the official explanation of the law. By detailed regulation, they brought the law within the reach of the understanding and obedience of ordinary men. But Jesus swept aside the tradition of the elders and restored the law to its true function as conveying to man God's intention for him. The scribes, however, saw this as endangering the law itself.

The Pharisees were the nationalists of the day. Their one dream was the restoration of the Jewish nation to freedom, and their one concern was the most careful preservation of every detail of Jewish practice in matters of religion and worship. Jesus seemed to them to be both irreverent and dangerous. The Romans had ordered that any Roman soldier could compel any Jew on the road to carry his pack for him one mile. Jesus said, "If this should happen to you, go not one mile but two" (see Matt. 5:41). It made the Pharisees' blood boil to hear such nonsense. Also, they had made the observance of the Sabbath the symbol of the keeping of the whole law; so that, when Jesus attacked the symbol, he naturally aroused their hatred. To the Pharisees, Jesus was an enemy of the nation on both counts.

The Herodians and the Zealots were the exact opposite of one another. The followers of Herod were the running-dogs of Rome. They were cunning in their cynical unconcern. Jesus nailed them to history with one word when he said of Herod, "Go and tell that fox" (Luke 13:32). The Zealots, on the other hand, were those who desired and sought to provoke or encourage an armed uprising against Rome. Barabbas was a Zealot, and Judas Iscariot also seems to have been sympathetic to the Zealot cause. The Herodians found that Jesus had a much clearer and more definite purpose than suited their idea of gently letting things go on as they were. The Zealots knew exactly what they wanted—an armed revolt; they could not understand why Jesus was so slow and hesitant. Jesus was too intense for the Herodians, and too obtuse for the Zealots. Both were glad to get rid of him.

And then, added to all these, was the scandal of Jesus' attitude to those men and women who were outside the pale of society. He befriended sinners—the common folk who were so slack about their religious practices; he forgave prostitutes—the objects of social contempt; he associated with publicans—servants of the Roman government who collected its taxes; he visited the Samaritans—who for centuries had been the enemies of the Jews; and he included in his mission the Gentiles—who were outside God's covenant with Abraham. Every known landmark was in danger because of Jesus.

Of course, it was true that Pilate had an unrepented past which tied his hands; that Caiaphas was avaricious, which confused his motives; that the scribes and the Pharisees sought acclaim, which dulled their vision; that Herod had lost his moral sense through his own cunning; and that the Zealots by their fanaticism had lost their capacity to love. All this was true; but Jesus was crucified not only because of all this evil in men but also because, as we have seen, this evil was

45

able to press into its service so much good. It was men in their devotion to good causes who crucified Jesus Christ; men in their concern for peace and order, for religion and freedom. Evil has little power in itself. It becomes powerful only when it is able to use what is good for its own purposes. That is why repentance, for us men, is such a difficult demand to meet; goodness and badness are so mixed up in us that it is not sufficient to repent for the bad; we have to recognize that even that in us which we consider good is constantly under the power of evil.

The Way the Story Is Told

We must now turn to trace the story of Jesus as the Gospels tell it; but, before we do this, two other preliminary points also need to be made: one is to make explicit the chronology we shall follow, and the other is to draw attention to a peculiarity in the way the Gospel story is told.

John sets the ministry of Jesus within the framework of four Passover feasts. The ministry begins with the cleansing of the temple at the first Passover, after which follows the main Galilean ministry. The second year begins with a controversy occasioned by the healing of the man at the pool of Bethzatha, which John says took place at a feast of the Jews. This controversy spreads to Galilee and continues throughout the year. The third year begins with the feeding of the five thousand, most of them pilgrims on their way to Jerusalem for the Passover. This third year Jesus spends mostly with his disciples. And the year comes to an end at the fourth Passover when Jesus is crucified.

As for the peculiarity of the way in which the Gospel story is told, the point can be made quite simply. On almost every page of the Gospel narrative, we shall find that there is the attempt of someone to answer the question, "Who is Jesus?" John the Baptist points to Jesus and says, "Behold, the Lamb of God!" (John 1:36). There is a voice from heaven which says, "This is my beloved Son" (Matt. 3:17). Nicodemus speaks to Jesus and says, "We know that you are a teacher come from God" (John 3:2). The Samaritan woman goes to her people and says, "Come, see. . . . Can this be the Christ?" (John 4:29). The demon-possessed man shouts out the words, "I know who you are, the Holy One of God" (Mark 1:24). And, against this stream of constant witnessing, the Gospels present Jesus as keeping the secret about himself. He does not say who he is, not to anyone. When, at Caesarea Philippi, Jesus asks the question directly of his disciples, "Who do you say that I am?" and Peter answers, "You are the Christ" (Mark 8:29), we recall the joy that welled up in the heart and voice of Jesus at the answer of Peter: "Blessed are you, Simon Bar-Jona! For flesh and blood has not revealed this to you, but my Father who is in heaven" (Matt. 16:17). Nevertheless, even after this incident the secret is still kept; for Jesus speaks now to his own disciples alone about who he is. Only when he stands bound and captive before the high priest and faces the prospect of the cross does he make public announcement of his identity. "Are you the Christ?" the high priest asks; to which the answer comes back like a pistol shot: "I am" (Mark 14:61-62; cf. Exod. 3:14). He who claims to be the Christ claims it at the very moment when he is at man's mercy, so that man is in a position to accept or reject that claim in freedom. Man's faith, uninfluenced by miracle, must make the discovery of who Jesus is.

Now for the story.

The Kingdom Is Announced—Hopeful Beginnings

It is harvest time in Judea when the Baptist appears on the bank of the river Jordan, clothed in hairy garment, the usual garb of a prophet since the days of Elijah, and demanding repentance from the people, for God's harvest time had come. Jesus joins John in this ministry, some of John's disciples attaching themselves to him. But this initial phase in the ministry of Jesus ends very quickly. He finds himself misunderstood by the disciples of John who imagine him to be a rival; so that he closes down his work in Judea and departs for Galilee. Indeed, the story breaks off at this point with the disciples of Jesus back in their homes and at their usual trades, and with Jesus himself back home in Capernaum with his mother. Here we leave Jesus for a time until we meet him again hurrying along the shore of the Sea of Galilee, recalling his disciples. News had come that Herod had cast John the Baptist into prison; but, before the people could be dismayed by the shock of this event, they were being caught and held by Jesus. He comes into Galilee, preaching and saying, "The time is fulfilled, and the kingdom of God is at hand; repent, and believe in the gospel" (Mark 1:14-15).

The ministry of Jesus in Galilee which opens with this declaration proceeds then to demonstrate its truth. As Jesus himself expressed it, his work was to bind the strong man of the house and take away his possessions (Mark 3:27). The opening incident in John's Gospel is the cleansing of the temple. Here begins the controversy that rages through his whole ministry. Luke opens his narrative with the synagogue incident in Nazareth. The stress here falls on who Jesus is. Also, here is struck the first note on the theme of the rejection of Israel which later finds its full amplification in the parable of the wicked husbandmen. Matthew's Gospel opens with the Sermon on the Mount—a greater than Moses is here; while the record in Mark opens with a series of five miracles of healing—the new age has dawned.

But this first period in the ministry of Jesus, the period of great hope, when the crowds listened to him with interest, when they wondered at his words of charm, and when they marveled at his authority, soon came to an end. Dawn turned to noon, and the springing plants began to wilt in the noonday heat.

The Church Disapproves—the Gathering Storm

The trouble began at Jerusalem. Jesus had gone there for the feast and, at the pool of Bethzatha, healed on the Sabbath day a man who had been ill for thirty-eight years. The controversy about the Sabbath is one of the central controversies in the Gospel story. It was fundamentally a controversy about the nature of God. To those for whom the Sabbath was the central symbol of their religious devotion, God was almost exclusively in the past tense. He had spoken, he had acted, he had revealed what man must do in response; man's religious duty simply lay in doing it. But Jesus was speaking of a Father in the present tense, at work still, whose demand of men was fellowship and cooperation in what he was continuing to do. This conflict of Jesus with the leaders of his people did not stop at Jerusalem; it followed him on his return to Galilee; and soon the complexion of his ministry there too was changed. The crowds who had followed him became the onlookers of a growing strife.

The primary conflict of Jesus was with the chief authorities of the Jewish church. He challenged the authority of the high priest by clearing the temple market. He challenged the authority of the scribes by setting aside the "tradition of the elders." He challenged the authority of the Pharisees by breaking the Sabbath rules. No wonder they all challenged him to state his credentials. "By what authority are you doing these things?" Do you have any certificate from any reputed rabbi? Is it not true that you have had no systematic training in theology? (Mark 11:28; John 2:18, 7:15.) There should be no surprise for us in this attempt on the part of those in authority to find out what the credentials of Jesus were. That was their business. It was precisely for this purpose that they held responsibility.

But there was also a secondary conflict which Jesus had to face—a conflict with the ordinary church members. The authorities were worried about his credentials, these were worried about his commonness. "He eats with publicans and sinners," was their complaint. The answer of Jesus was that this was not really true. He did not eat with publicans as such; he ate with Matthew and his friends, with Zacchaeus and his family. He did not consort with sinners as sinners. He just befriended this particular woman who was caught in adultery, and that particular woman who anointed his feet, and that particular man whose sin had paralyzed his body. It is we men who think of people as types. They are colored and we are white; they are Jews and we are Arabs; they are men and we are women; they are Roman Catholics and we are Protestants. Jesus thought of people as persons.

The Sadducees defending the temple, the Pharisees defending the law, the scribes defending the tradition, the people defending their respectability—all were ranged against Jesus, and Jesus was ranged against them. How would it end?

Jesus Replies—the New Community

The situation reached a point of complete confusion quite early in the second year of Jesus' ministry. As the Gospels portray it, the people were, in one way or another, charmed by his grace, amazed by his power, struck by his authority, perplexed by his reticence, offended by his commonness, and doubtful about his claims. In this situation, the leaders spread abroad a more or less official answer to Jesus. They announced that whatever authority and power he had was of the devil (Matt. 12:24), that he was really only an impostor without any credentials (John 9:29), and that in any case he was lowborn and uneducated (John 7:15). We know this man, they said: he is a carpenter and the son of a carpenter; we also know his mother and his sisters (Mark 6:3); and we hardly need to add that we were not born of fornication (John 8:41).

The reply of Jesus to this attitude of the leaders of his people was a striking one. Here is how Luke records it: "But they were filled with fury and discussed with one another what they might do to Jesus. In these days he went out into the hills to pray; and all night he continued in prayer to God. And when it was day, he called his disciples and chose from them twelve" (Luke 6:11-13). The significance of that number "twelve" could not have been lost either on the friends or on the enemies of Jesus. Here was the nucleus of the new Ecclesia, the new chosen people of God. The vineyard was being handed over to new husbandmen (Matt. 21:41). Luke adds two other features as belonging to the reply of Jesus. He tells us that Jesus changed his mode of public teaching, speaking hereafter largely in the form of parables; and that he also undertook and carried out an active and urgent ministry through the cities and villages of Galilee. The purpose of Jesus in speaking in parables is explained as an attempt to state the truth in a form which faith alone could grasp, as well as in a form which the hearer would not easily forget, so that it remained in the memory available for the apprehension of faith.

When the enemies of Jesus saw that they had failed in drawing the crowds away from Jesus, and in frightening Jesus himself, they tried a second method of keeping him quiet. Jesus seemed to them to be every day more sure of his purpose and more careless of consequences; while the crowd was less willing to disbelieve in him, having become ever more deeply impressed by the kind of miracles which he had lately performed. He had raised from the dead a young man who was being taken for burial (Luke 7:11-17); and he had ordered the cure of a common servant of a Roman centurion, a Gentile, even without going to the house where the servant was (Luke 7:1-10). The crowds saw in Jesus a breadth and a power of love which it was not easy to deny. In this situation, where they were losing their initiative, what the enemies of Jesus did was to go to the brothers of Jesus. The brothers were already alarmed by Jesus' growing unpopularity, and it is possible also that they were suffering in their business because of the hostility of the leaders of the people to their brother. The Pharisees and scribes and Herodians come to them and say, "How is it that you are keeping quiet? Can't you see that Jesus is getting himself into trouble and will get you into trouble too? What he needs is a complete rest. He is overworking himself and has lost his balance." This is an account of an imaginary conversation. What we know for certain is that the brothers of Jesus went, taking Mary with them, to where Jesus was. They found him in the midst of a crowd and sent for him; but Jesus would not come to meet them. He sent them a significant reply: "Who is my mother, and who are my brothers?" And stretching out his hands toward his disciples he said, "Here are my mother and my brothers! For whoever does the will of my Father in heaven is my brother, and sister, and mother" (Matt. 12:46-50; cf. John 7:3).

The last and final attempt of the enemies of Jesus was to win him over with a show of favor. They had him invited to dinner by one of the important men of the place. The Pharisee Simon, a gem merchant, agreed to be host; but, while he was willing to invite Jesus as his guest, he was not willing to accord him all the courtesy which was a guest's by right. He gave him no water to wash his feet; he gave him neither the kiss of welcome nor the oil of anointing; and he seated him at the foot of the table near the door, and not next to the host, where the honored guest should sit. We know what happened at that meal. The woman who had been a sinner did for Jesus all that Simon had left undone and more. The direct words of Jesus to Simon followed: "I tell you, her sins, which are many, are forgiven, for she loved much; but he who is forgiven little, loves little" (Luke 7:47).

The Galilean ministry of Jesus now draws swiftly to its close; but one more incident must be recorded before the end. It is the incident of the message to Jesus of John the Baptist: "Are you he who is to come, or shall we look for another?" We know the answer of Jesus to John: "Go and tell John what you have seen and heard: the blind receive their sight, the lame walk, the lepers are cleansed, and the deaf hear, the dead are raised up, the poor have good news preached to them. And blessed is he who takes no offense at me" (Luke 7:22-23).

The Close of the Galilean Ministry—the Shadows Lengthen

The Galilean ministry now ends, and from now on Jesus no more conducts a public ministry in Galilee. He had worked here for a year and a half. The ministry had begun in great hope; it was closing amidst great conflict. And the last picture we see of Jesus, as he leaves the shores of Galilee, is the picture of him sitting in a boat in a bay of the sea speaking to the crowd. He is telling them some stories of harvest. A man sowed the seed, and then he did nothing more than sleep and wake and eat, and eat and sleep and wake; but the seed was living seed, so that it grew of itself—first the blade, then the ear, then the corn in the ear. The word of God is never wasted (Mark 4:26-29). There was another man who sowed wheat, and, behold, in his field grew up not merely wheat but tares. Should the tares be pulled up? No. Let them grow together until the harvest, and then the wheat will be gathered and the tares burnt. Evil flourishes only for a time. Judgment will soon overtake it. Nor can it prevent the good from coming to its harvest (Matt. 13:24-30). And yet there is no harvest without waste of some of the seed that is sown. A sower went forth to sow and, as he sowed, some of the seed fell by the wayside, and the birds of the air carried them away. Some seed fell on rocky ground. They grew, but the plants soon withered under the heat of the sun. Some seed fell among thorns, and though they grew, the thorns too grew and choked them. But some seed fell on good ground, and these yielded a good harvest, some thirtyfold, some sixtyfold, and some a hundredfold. The Pharisees may not listen; the response of the crowd may be superficial; even so faithful a servant as John the Baptist may doubt; the brothers of Jesus may be frightened; but the seed has been sown, and harvest time will surely come (Mark 4:3-20).

So the day ends, and as the crowds disperse talking among themselves about the meaning of his stories, Jesus himself lies down in the boat and goes to sleep. He is tired, body and soul; and the disciples row him across the lake. "They took him . . . as he was" is the comment of the Gospel writer (Mark 4:36).

The second part of the second year of Jesus' ministry was mainly occupied with the training of the disciples. They must be prepared for the decisive struggle that lay ahead. The sequence of events is fairly clear. On the way across the lake a storm arises; but Jesus awakes from his sleep, and shows himself in command of the situation. Not only is the storm stilled but the faith of his disciples is steadied. On the eastern side of the lake, in the land of Gadara, Jesus meets and cures a demoniac. This man desires to follow Jesus, but is told to go home and tell his people the news of what God has done for him (Mark 5:19). Jesus himself, however, has to leave the place because the people begged him to do so. They had lost their pigs, and were afraid of the losses which they might have to suffer because of Jesus. So Jesus comes once more to the Galilean side of the lake. Here he is called upon to heal the daughter of Jairus, one of the rulers of the synagogue. The daughter dies before Jesus can come to her. But Jesus comes, nevertheless, and raises her from the dead. To Peter, James, and John this must have been a turning point in their experience. Then comes Jesus' visit to Nazareth, his hometown. He has come to say good-bye. But his townsmen are so angered by his teaching that they attempt to throw him down the hill and kill him. Jesus, perceiving their intention, turns round and faces them; and they fall back, allowing him to go away unharmed. There was that in his face which they could not withstand. The rejection of Jesus by the people of Nazareth is the final end of the Galilean story, and the lament of Jesus over the Galilean towns expressed his sorrow that this story should have ended thus:

Woe to you, Chorazin! Woe to you, Bethsaida! for if the mighty works done in you had been done in Tyre and Sidon, they would have repented long ago in sackcloth and ashes. But I tell you, it shall be more tolerable on that day of judgment for Tyre and Sidon than for you. And you, Capernaum, will you be exalted to

heaven? You shall be brought down to Hades. For if the mighty
works done in you had been done in Sodom, it would have remained until this day. (Matt. 11:21-23.)

The Beginning of the End

Suddenly, like thunder across the darkened sky, came the
news that John the Baptist had been beheaded. It was the
sign of the shadow of the cross. From this time Jesus began
to speak to his disciples about the suffering that was bound to
come upon him, and to teach them that they too must be
prepared to face persecution. "Whoever does not bear his own
cross and come after me," he said, "cannot be my disciple."
(Luke 14:27.)

In the Gospel records not much is said about the planning
and plotting which the enemies of Jesus carried on as they
prepared the means for getting rid of him. All that we know
is that such planning and plotting went on. There was the
desire to have Jesus waylaid and killed quietly (John 7:1).
There was the attempt to have witnesses ready to accuse him
if he was ever brought to trial (John 8:6). There was all the
discussion among themselves that was necessary to ensure that
such different and rival groups as the Sadducees, the Pharisees, and the Herodians should act together (Mark 3:6).
There was the need too to get the Sanhedrin, some of the
members of which were friendly with Jesus, convinced that
it was essential that he should now be destroyed (John 7:
50-52). And finally, there was the need to get someone from
among those who were nearest to Jesus to give them informa-
tion as to the attitude of Jesus himself to the fast-developing

situation (Matt. 26:14-16). In the name of all that they held dear, the enemies of Jesus saw no way out of their difficulties except to destroy him.

The first move of Jesus as he prepared for the final conflict was to send out his disciples on a mission on their own. That was the only way for them to find out what it meant to say that the kingdom of God had come. It was also his last attempt to win the lost house of Israel. As the disciples went to carry out their commission, Jesus himself retired across the lake to spend time in quiet with his Father. The disciples returned to him after a successful tour. Jesus took them and went with them apart to rest awhile (Mark 6:31). A crowd, many of them on their way to the Passover, found Jesus here on the eastern side of the lake, where he was with his disciples. They had gathered around him, and he taught them. Soon it was evening, and they had had nothing to eat the whole day. Jesus himself fed them, using a few loaves and fishes which a lad among them had brought. The crowd went wild with excitement because of what Jesus had done. Even the disciples were excited. They were already full of the enthusiasm caused by their experience on the mission from which they had just returned. So they and the crowd together suddenly surged around Jesus and asked him to be their king (John 6:15). When Jesus had been tempted in the wilderness, at the very outset of his ministry, and had rejected every suggestion of the devil, the Gospel record says, "The devil . . . departed from him until an opportune time (Luke 4:13). He came back now with just the same temptation—bread, excitement, compromise. The answer of Jesus was decisive. He refused the crown; he sent back the crowd; he hurried his disciples into a boat and ordered them across the lake, while he himself went alone to pray.

We meet Jesus again after this, walking on the water to his disciples. It is a perfect picture of the moment at which his ministry has arrived: a howling wind, a raging sea, a moonless night, a group of frightened men in a tossing boat, weary of rowing—and Jesus the master of wind and wave. Peter says to him, "Lord, . . . bid me come to you on the water." And Jesus says, "Come." Peter steps out, sinks for a moment, and is saved (Matt. 14:25-33).

We leave the story at this point to pick it up again; and, as we leave it, pray Peter's prayer, "Lord, bid me come to you on the water." Those who find faith find it only because faith has become necessary. It is not really necessary as long as one is in the boat.

CHAPTER 3

In the way in which I have been telling the story, the emphasis has been on listening to the story as a whole. This does not mean that there is no other way of dealing with the story. Indeed, in the first place, the story as it is told in each Gospel is the result of assembling together discrete parts of the oral tradition; each part in this tradition being normally composed of a remembered saying or incident in the life of Jesus together with the preaching or teaching of it.

An essential part of the study of the Gospels, therefore, has to be to look at each piece of the oral tradition, to assess its probable accuracy, and to see how homiletic or apologetic reasons have affected the way in which a saying or an incident has been remembered. It will also be an essential part of the study to find out what it is that is actually sought to be conveyed, so that it is understood in the way that is most meaningful to the listener now.

However, this study of the parts by themselves cannot convey what the parts together mean. Another method is necessary for this, and I know of no way of explaining this method except to say that one must expose oneself to the story as a whole and seek to take one's own place in that story. This method may be described as that of intelligent imagination, but it is not simply that. Its foundation is the continuing presence and ministry of the risen Lord. For Jesus Christ is risen, and our Christmas is always after Easter.

WHAT HAPPENED? THE STORY THE GOSPELS TELL (II)

The Gospel writers have a purpose, and that purpose has determined both what they have selected to record and the way in which they have recorded it. As the Fourth Evangelist puts it: "Now Jesus did many other signs in the presence of the disciples, which are not written in this book; but these are written that you may believe that Jesus is the Christ, the Son of God, and that believing you may have life in his name" (John 20:30-31). It is by this purpose of the evangelist, then, that we are controlled as we continue with this story. We too are included in the concern that those who read or listen should find faith.

The Third Year—Both Sides Prepare for the Conflict

The point in the story at which we have arrived is the break that has taken place between Jesus and the leaders of his people. We now follow the consequences of that break as Jesus prepares for the final conflict.

His first act, at this point in the story, was to get rid of all "passengers"—that is, all on whom he could not count to be faithful to the end. His teaching took on a quality of depth and difficulty which soon caused those who were merely interested to turn back and follow him no more. In fact, even the disciples began to waver. But one direct question from Jesus rallied them again: "Will you also go away?" he asked; and Peter replied for them all when he said, "Lord to whom shall we go? You have the words of eternal life" (John 6:66-68). Jesus then took his disciples and went away quietly to far-off Phoenicia. There he was not known, and he hoped to be able to spend unhurried time with them. But he was soon discovered, and a woman of Phoenicia came to him for help. Jesus asked her, "Is it right to take the children's bread and give it to the dogs, even if they be pet dogs?" The woman answered the kindly glance of Jesus' eye, rather than his words, when she replied, "No, master, but the children themselves give of their bread to their pets." She got what she wanted, but Jesus was unable to have quiet in Phoenicia any more (Matt. 15:21-28). So he hurried across the whole length of Galilee and came again to the eastern side of the Jordan to the land of the Decapolis (Mark 7:31). But here, the man who had been set free from the legion of devils which troubled him had obeyed so well the command of Jesus to tell others all that God had done for him that, the moment it was known that Jesus was in Decapolis, crowds came to him. Jesus left at once, and this time went quietly to Galilee itself. However, here again he was soon discovered, and the waverers among the scribes and Pharisees came to him with a last request. They too were constantly puzzled by Jesus—by the sureness with which he spoke and worked, and yet the restraint which seemed to hold him back from taking advantage of his success. Jesus answered their request for a sign with a blunt refusal. His works themselves were signs if only they would read them. But to those who would not see, no sign could be given. Besides, why was not the sign which Jonah gave to the Ninevites enough for them? Jonah gave no sign except the message which he proclaimed: "Forty days and forty nights and this city will be destroyed" (see Jonah 3:4). And the Ninevites believed and repented. Could the Jews not see that the signs of judgment were all around them too? When the sky was red in the evening, they could tell that it would be fair weather; and when it was red in the morning, they could tell that it would be stormy. Why not similarly read the signs of the times? To ask for a sign in spite of all this was to show that they were divided in their own minds and were not willing to give their whole loyalty to Jesus. Only an adulterous people would ask for a sign to make sure who their legitimate lord was (Matt. 16:1-12).

After this conversation Jesus did not linger in Galilee any more. He took his disciples and went north. The town to which they came was Caesarea Philippi. Here Jesus finally led the disciples to face the one issue on which all depended. Did his disciples know him, know who he was? They may not

63

have understood everything he said or did. They never would. But who did they think he was? Simon Peter jumped over all the hurdles of their doubt in one grand leap. Who would ask the question about himself except the One who had the right to make that his question? "You are the Christ," he said, "the Son of the living God" (Matt. 16:16). The living God—that was the God of their Scriptures; the God who called Abraham, the God who sent Moses, the God who chose David as king; and Jesus was his Christ, his anointed, his Son; the One to whom the Scriptures pointed, the One in whom the promise of the Scriptures was fulfilled.

No sooner had Peter declared the identity of Jesus than Jesus began to speak about the sufferings he had to undergo and the death he must die. He had perceived how the Messiah of the apocalypse and the Suffering Servant of prophecy were one. But to the disciples this talk of suffering, so soon after the exultation attending Peter's confession, was completely confusing. They could not understand it. And Peter expressed their mind with his usual vigor when he rebuked his Master. "What you say cannot be, it does not make sense," was what he said. Jesus said to him, "Peter, the foundation stone should not become the stone of stumbling. As long as you see things only in their natural light, and talk as men talk, then you are an instrument of the devil himself. Suffering is the royal road of the Messiah and of his people" (see Matt. 16:13-23).

Peter and his friends were silenced, but they still did not understand. Soon, however, they were to have another experience. Jesus took them with him up on the mountain to pray. Nine of the disciples stayed farther down, while Peter, James, and John went with their Master to the top. There they saw a vision of his glory. Moses and Elijah were there speaking with Jesus about the "decease which he must accomplish at Jerusalem." His suffering and death were a task to be accomplished, not an infliction to be endured. Both the law and the prophets pointed to it. So did the disciples catch a glimmer of the truth that the glory of the Son was the glorious splendor of love poured out (Matt. 17:1-8).

There are three predictions which Jesus makes of his passion and, as the Gospel records show, these reveal the way in which the situation was developing. The first prediction, made at Caesarea Philippi (Matt. 16:21), indicates the probability of action by the Sanhedrin, the Council of the Jews. The second prediction, made on the way to Jerusalem (Luke 17: 25, cf. John 11:8), speaks of the possibility of Jesus being secretly killed by his enemies. And the third prediction, made on the way to the Passover feast itself (Matt. 20:18-19; 26:2), points to crucifixion by the Romans. The enemies of Jesus were at work all the time; and Jesus was not unaware of their plans.

The Bid for Jerusalem—into the Jaws of Death

The Gospel picture of Jesus as he turns his face toward Jerusalem is a striking one. Caesarea Philippi and the mount of transfiguration were enough to hold the faith of the disciples. Indeed, the disciples were now so sure about the triumph of Jesus that they had begun to quarrel among themselves as to how they would share the honors of his kingdom. But Jesus was walking on ahead, his face steadfastly set toward Jerusalem. How symbolic this picture is, and how sorrowfully true so often—Jesus on his way to the cross, and the church behind him arguing about place and influence!

Peter seems to have been the chief object of jealousy in the quarrel among the disciples. He was so deeply upset that he asked Jesus how many times he should forgive, or whether at any stage he could declare an open breach and be done with it (Matt. 18:21-22). Later on James and John entered the picture by bringing to Jesus their mother, who asked him to grant special places to her sons in the coming kingdom (Matt. 20:20-23). It was perhaps at this time also that there happened the incident of the thirteenth man. It was bad enough having twelve people among whom to distribute the honors; to have a thirteenth added was worse. John said to Jesus, "We saw a man casting out demons in your name, and we forbade him, because he was not following us." Jesus replied, "Do not forbid him. . . . For he that is not against us is for us" (Mark 9:38-40).

Jesus had not got beyond Galilee on his way to Jerusalem before the Pharisees and scribes came to him with the request that he pay his temple tax. Herod had built and completed the temple of Jerusalem, but every Jew had to pay a tax to wipe out the debt on it, and for its upkeep. Would Jesus pay? Jesus immediately arranged for the tax to be paid, for he did not want to give his enemies the chance of accusing him of disloyalty to their faith (Matt. 17:24-27). He would himself choose the hour and the mode of the final conflict between them. The initiative would be his to the very end.

Jesus now entered Samaria. But, since he was going to Jerusalem, the Samaritan village in which they sought to rest for the night would not receive them. James and John were so indignant that they wanted to call down fire from heaven to destroy the village. Jesus merely passed on (Luke 9:51-56). He was on his way to Jerusalem and nothing would distract him. He must not dally in the way, nor allow side-issues to delay him; he just went straight ahead. The parables he tells his disciples on the way are also significant. They are all parables about preparedness and of the grounds for hope. Early in his ministry in Galilee, his parables were about the nature of the kingdom; then in the midst of the gathering conflict he had told them the parables of harvest and the crisis of judgment; and now on the way to Jerusalem he was exhorting them to be ready for any emergency. The absent master will come when least expected; the delay of the bridegroom must be prepared for; it will not be enough for servants to be careful, they will need to be alert (Mark 13: 34-37; Matt. 25:1-13, 14-30). Also, for this preparedness there are sure grounds of hope: for the kingdom of heaven is like a grain of mustard seed that is sown (Luke 13:18-19); it is like a lump of leaven that is mixed (Luke 13:20-21); it is also like a city set on a hill (Matt. 5:14). The smallness of the seed, the silence of the leaven, the distance of the city, are no cause for depression or despair. The seed will grow; the leaven will continue to work; the city will remain.

When Jesus arrived in Jerusalem, the chief priests and the Pharisees sent officers to arrest him. It is true that the officers came back without fulfilling their commission and saying, "No man ever spoke like this man!" (John 7:46); but Jesus himself did not receive any general response. So he departed from their midst and went across the Jordan to Perea. He was in Perea for about three months until the feast of the Dedication, when he came to Jerusalem again. This time, he was involved in another bitter controversy which arose as a result of his healing a man who was blind from his birth. The words of Jesus at the climax of that controversy, during which they even tried to stone him, are significant. He said to the man who was healed, "For judgment I came into this world, that those who do not see may see, and that those who see may become blind." Some of the Pharisees near him heard this, and they said to him, "Are we also blind?" Jesus said to them, "If you were blind, you would have no guilt; but now that you say, 'We see,' your guilt remains." (John 9:39-41.)

This whole period of Jesus' ministry in Jerusalem which was marked by persistent conflict with the leaders of his people was also marked by the most forthright teaching which he gave about himself. However, they did not understand. So that there was one last attempt which they made to find out exactly what he was trying to say. They said to him, "How long will you keep us in suspense? If you are the Christ, tell us plainly." Jesus answered them, "My sheep hear my voice, and I know them, and they follow me; and I give them eternal life. . . . My Father, who has given them to me, is greater than all, and no one is able to snatch them out of the Father's hand. I and the Father are one." (John 10:24-30.) That was the end. He had made his final assertion, and they made their final rejection. A second time they took up stones to stone him; but he went away from their midst, and was in Perea until he came to Jerusalem for the last time for the Passover.

The Perean Interlude—Jesus Chooses His Hour

The ministry of Jesus in Perea, which lasted from the feast of Tabernacles to the feast of Dedication, and then from the feast of Dedication to the feast of the Passover, is recorded for us primarily in the Gospel according to Luke. It was a ministry of Jesus to all people without any distinction. From Galilee he had sent out his twelve disciples to the lost house of Israel; from Perea he sent out seventy disciples to all the nations (Luke 10:1-17). It was a common notion that Israel consisted of twelve tribes and the world consisted of seventy nations. Also to the Perean ministry belong those parables of Jesus which deal with the cost of discipleship: the story of the man who began to build a tower but could not complete it, and the story of the king who went to war without reckoning the strength of his enemy (Luke 14:28-32); also the parables about the lost sons, the lost sheep, and the lost coin (Luke 15:4-32); and finally, the parables about the right attitude to worldly wealth—such as the story of the intelligent rogue and of the rich man and Lazarus (Luke 16:1-9, 19-31).

Clearly the intention of Jesus was to stay on in Perea up to the time of the Passover. The Jews had sought to stone him, but his end would not take the form of that kind of death at the hands of a mob, or of secret assassination. His people as a whole must make their decision about him, and Jesus had decided how to face them with that moment of decision. So he waited in Perea. But suddenly news came that his friend Lazarus was ill. He did not go. Then the news came that Lazarus was dead. He must go. His disciples were taken aback by his decision to go to Bethany. But they saw that his mind was made up and that nothing would stop his going. Thomas said to the rest, "Let us also go, that we may die with him." Jesus came to Bethany. We know the sequel. Lazarus was raised to life again (John 11:1-44). Immediately there was a new enthusiasm in the crowd for Jesus; but Jesus knew how fickle that crowd could be. Besides, this event of the raising of Lazarus made it very clear to the leaders of the Jews that they must act quickly. They too could not depend on the crowd. They must make the crowd act according to their will before Jesus had time to press home his advantage and secure a permanent and unshakable loyalty. Jesus did not return to Perea by the way he had come. He slipped away north to the little village of Ephraim, and when everything was quiet went back again beyond Jordan. There he remained until his final journey to Jerusalem.

Soon it was the time of the Passover. So Jesus collected his disciples and set out for the city. His mind and soul were full of the tragedy that lay ahead of him. He was going to Jerusalem to accomplish his death. On the way three men came to him and offered to follow him. The first was anxious to share in the great happenings that were evidently to take place in Jerusalem. Jesus said to him, "I do not want anyone to do great deeds on my behalf. All I want now is quiet and restful companionship and friendship, somewhere for the Son of man to lay his head." The would-be disciple turned away. He had offered to join in an adventure. He had no time or taste for quiet friendship. Another came up and said, "I will go with you, but not now. I have duties at home to ful-

70

fill. I have an old father whom I must look after till his death."
Jesus said to him, "Let the dead bury the dead. There are
always enough people to attend to the business of this world;
you follow me." But the man would not. Jesus turned to a
third man who seemed to be interested in the conversation and
said to him, "Will you follow?" The man answered, "Yes—but
I must run home first and say good-bye." Jesus said to him, "I
cannot wait here for you until you go home and say good-bye.
For no man puts his hand to the plow and turns back, not
even to wait for a would-be disciple." (See Luke 9:57-62.)

Jesus must hasten on, for the hour had come. But, at this
stage, it was still his purpose to go quietly; his enemies must
not know what his movements were. This explains why the
disciples were so anxious to stop the shouting of Bartimaeus
(Luke 18:35-39). The story of Zacchaeus closes the narrative.
It is the last incident before Jesus comes to Bethany (Luke
19:1-10). And so, as Luke has it, the story of the public ministry of Jesus ends, closing with the words of invitation addressed to Zacchaeus: "Make haste and come down; for I must
stay at your house today." There is now only one week more,
the week of the final tragedy and triumph.

The Last Week—the Way of the Cross

We read the story of the cross and all that led up to it from
the vantage point of the resurrection of Christ. We know that
he is risen. But those who followed him during the last week
of tragedy in Jerusalem did not know. His friends and disciples
followed, hardly knowing what to expect—and their mood at

71

the end of it all is well expressed in those words of the disciples on their way to Emmaus: "We thought that he was to be the Savior of Israel, but he is dead" (see Luke 24:21).

Our attempt in this narrative must be simply to follow the incidents of this week as they happened, and try to see them with the eyes of his first disciples. Indeed, the incidents so crowd upon one another, and each so tells its own story, that little comment on them is necessary. We shall merely recount them, remembering that, as we follow Jesus here, we are following him to his cross and to our own.

The Jewish day is from sunset to sunset, so that we shall look at the events of each day during this last week according to this time reckoning.

On Sunday, Jesus has his evening meal, which, according to our time reckoning will be Saturday evening, in the home of the family at Bethany. It is at this meal when, after the anointing by Mary, Jesus speaks openly about his death, and Judas finally resolves to precipitate the issue by betraying him. In the early morning, Jesus leaves for Jerusalem riding on an ass. It is a quiet and thoughtful procession. The figure of Jesus riding on an ass raises questions that for long have remained unasked. Is he really the long expected king? As Jesus nears Jerusalem, a crowd of Galileans who are in Jerusalem hear about his coming and go out to meet him. They escort him into the city in triumphal procession. As Jesus turns the bend on the road and Jerusalem comes into view, he dismounts. Tears roll down his face. "O Jerusalem, Jerusalem," he cries, "How often I would . . . and you would not." Jesus enters Jerusalem and goes into the temple. He looks round about upon everything. He withdraws for the night to Bethany.

On Monday, Jesus leaves in the morning again for Jerusalem. On the way he tells the story of the fig tree which, when no one would have expected fruit from it since it was not the season for figs, nevertheless deceived people into expecting non-seasonal fruit because it had leaves. Whether this parable was also actually enacted we cannot tell. The story ends in Mark's Gospel with the words, "May no one ever eat fruit from you again." Within forty years, Jerusalem and its temple were in ruins. On entering Jerusalem, Jesus goes into the temple. The children, seeing him, take up the cry of the previous day, "Hosanna to the Son of David." The chief priests and scribes seek to prevent the children from acclaiming him. He replies, quoting words of scripture, "Out of the mouths of babes and sucklings thou hast brought perfect praise." He spends the rest of the day in the temple precincts teaching and healing, returning in the evening to Bethany.

On Tuesday, when Jesus returns to Jerusalem, his enemies are waiting for him in the temple court. They have prepared three questions with which to trap him: (1) an ecclesiastical question—By what authority?—an answer to which they hope will get Jesus into difficulty with the Jewish authorities (Matt. 21:23-27); (2) a political question—Is it lawful to give tribute to Caesar?—an answer to which they hope will get Jesus into difficulty with the Roman authorities (Matt. 22:15-22); (3) a theological question—How shall it be in the resurrection?—an answer to which they hope will discredit Jesus in the eyes of the common people (Matt. 22:23-33).

The answers of Jesus confound them.

A bystander then asks a fourth question: "Which is the great commandment?" Jesus announces the double commandment, "Love God and love your neighbor also." Then follow three parables to explain how and why God will set aside his first choice of Israel: the story of the two sons and their obedience, the story of the husbandmen who attempted to make the vineyard theirs, and the story of the man without his wedding garment (Matt. 21:28-22:14). The Master's last word spoken in the temple is in praise of a widow whose gift he notices. "They all contributed out of their abundance," he says, "but she out of her poverty has put in everything she had, her whole living." In the afternoon Jesus leaves the temple courts, crosses the brook Kidron, and goes to the Mount of Olives. He sits there with his disciples and tells them about the things which still lie in the future.

On Wednesday, Jesus stays at Bethany. He will not go to Jerusalem again to preach or teach. In the morning a group of people seek him out at Bethany. These are Jewish proselytes or inquirers from the Greek-speaking towns, perhaps Alexandria, who have come to Jerusalem for the feast. They are impressed by Jesus, and they now come to him in private to request him to go with them. Why must he stay in Jerusalem and die? The disciples bring Jesus this message from the Greeks. Jesus comes out to meet them. His answer to them is to point to a truth enshrined in the very process of nature. "Unless a grain of wheat falls into the earth and dies," he says to them, "it remains alone; but if it dies, it bears much fruit." But the request of these Greeks does force into the foreground again the question: Must this be? Is this the only way? In the record of the Fourth Evangelist, this moment is set down as a dialogue in the mind of the Master. "Now is my soul troubled. And what shall I say, 'Father, save me from this hour'? No, for this purpose I have come to this hour. Father, glorify thy name."

On Thursday, Judas goes to the chief priests and makes his bargain with them. The Sanhedrin meets and the decision is taken to kill Jesus. It is not improbable that there were those in the Sanhedrin who were sympathetic to Jesus—Nicodemus, for instance; for when Jesus is arrested Caiaphas is unable to do without Jewish legal formalities. There must have been those who insisted on a fair trial with witnesses to prove the charges against him.

In the late morning, Jesus sends two of his disciples to the city to prepare what is to be his last meal with them. The house in which this supper is arranged is in all probability the home of John Mark, a nephew of Peter. As Thursday draws to a close, Jesus sets out with his disciples to Jerusalem. The moment has come for the final sacrifice.

On Friday, it is a crowded story. The Gospel writers narrate the events of this day as having taken place successively in seven places: the Upper Room, the garden of Gethsemane, the high priest's palace, the proconsul's court, the way to Calvary, Calvary itself, and the garden where Jesus was buried. Let us follow the events in this order.

Who Is This Jesus?

In the Upper Room

The disciples understand so little of the nature of the kingdom that Jesus had come to establish that even at this last moment, on their way to Jerusalem, they quarrel about first places. The result is that they enter the Upper Room without washing each other's feet, as custom and courtesy demanded. Jesus notices, but says nothing. He himself washes the disciples' feet, and thus plays the part of the servant to his brethren. The meal follows. Jesus makes his last appeal to Judas, and then gives him a chance to go without being suspected by the rest. The New Covenant is instituted in the breaking of the bread and the sharing of the cup. The gift of peace, the promise of the Spirit, the hymn of praise—and the farewell meal is over. Jesus and his disciples cross the Kidron valley into the garden of Gethsemane.

In the Garden of Gethsemane

When he arrives at the garden he takes Peter, James, and John with him, leaving the others near the entrance. Farther on, he leaves these three disciples also, and goes ahead alone to pray, with the request that they too keep awake and pray for him. But they fall asleep because they are sad.

Christ's agony in Gethsemane is one of the most difficult things to understand. His disciples, after him, met death and suffering with less conflict of spirit and a more serene peace. Why was Jesus so troubled? Have we here an indication of what it must have meant to him who had no sin to carry the guilt of the sin which plotted his death? Judas comes to Jesus with the temple guard to effect his arrest. Peter slashes out, perhaps at Judas, and cuts off the ear of a servant of the high priest. Jesus rebukes Peter and heals the servant's ear. He saves his disciples from being arrested. They run away. He is arrested and taken to the palace of the high priest.

In the High Priest's Palace

Peter enters with the rest. His Galilean speech betrays him. He denies knowledge of his Master. Jesus looks at him. He goes out and weeps bitterly. "Simon, Simon, behold, Satan demanded to have you, that he might sift you like wheat, but I have prayed for you that your faith may not fail; and when you have turned again, strengthen your brethren." (Luke 22:31-32.)

Jesus is first taken to Annas, the father-in-law of the high priest, and is questioned by him. Jesus tells him that it is not necessary to question him directly, since he has always spoken and acted in public. Correct legal procedure demanded the examination of witnesses. Jesus is struck by the bystanders. He is then taken to Caiaphas, who calls witnesses, and proceeds to conduct the trial according to the legal procedure laid down. (It is interesting to note this aspect of legality in the arrest and trial of Jesus, when so much of it was illegal. It was illegal for the temple guard to effect the arrest. The witnesses themselves should produce the accused. It was illegal to try a capital charge by night. It was illegal, when the testimony of the witnesses had broken down, for the judge to cross-examine the prisoner directly. And yet, the legal procedure followed at the trial shows that Caiaphas was not all-powerful to work his will that night.) The witnesses did not agree. Caiaphas addresses Jesus directly, "Are you the Christ, the Son of the Blessed?" "I AM." It was the first plain declaration in public of his Messiahship. Jesus is found guilty and condemned to death. He is struck, spat upon, and buffeted.

In the Proconsul's Court

Some three hours seem to have elapsed between the departure of Judas from the Upper Room to the house of the high priest and the actual arrest of Jesus in Gethsemane. This delay may well have been due to the fact that Caiaphas had to make arrangements with Pilate beforehand. What these arrangements were, we shall see as the story develops.

Pilate leaves his apartments early to receive the prisoner. His wife finds him already gone when she awakes. She sends word to him not to fulfill his promise to Caiaphas, which must have been to ratify formally the sentence of Caiaphas on Jesus. Pilate comes out of the court, without objection, to receive the accused and his accusers. The Jews could not go into the court, for there would have been no time later to purify themselves before the feast. When, in response to his wife's note, Pilate shows that he intends to retry the prisoner, Caiaphas shows his resentment; "If this man were not an evildoer," he says, "we would not have handed him over." But Pilate is adamant.

The trial before Pilate is long and arduous. He seeks to

shift responsibility onto the high priest or Herod. At last he yields, and in response to the cry, "We have no king but Caesar," hands Jesus over to be crucified. It is an irony of history that the people whose watchword was "We have no king but God" deny this fundamental principle of their national and religious life in order to have Jesus crucified.

The Way of the Cross

Jesus has been scourged and crowned with thorns. They have robed him in purple and mocked him as king. Now they put on him his own garments and lead him out to be crucified. He goes bearing his cross, but it is too heavy for his lacerated back to bear. They meet an African—Simon of Cyrene—and compel him to carry the cross of Jesus. Two robbers who are to be crucified with him follow, each carrying his own cross. A great crowd follows, and many women weep. Jesus turns to them saying: "Daughters of Jerusalem, do not weep for me, but weep for yourselves and for your children. For behold, the days are coming when they will say, 'Blessed are the barren, and the wombs that never bore, and the breasts that never gave suck!' Then they will begin to say to the mountains, 'Fall on us'; and to the hills, 'Cover us.' For if they do this when the wood is green, what will happen when it is dry?" (Luke 23:28-31).

The procession passes out of the city gates to the hill beyond and when they reach Golgotha—the place of the skull —they make ready to crucify Jesus. The cross is placed on the ground, and Jesus is stretched upon it. They offer him wine mixed with myrrh to numb his senses; but he refuses to drink it. As the nails are driven into his flesh, he prays, "Father forgive them; for they know not what they do." The cross is now raised upright and placed in its socket. Jesus is crucified. He saved others; he could not save himself.

Calvary

There are seven words of Jesus spoken from the cross which are recorded in the Gospel story. As he is crucified, he prays for those who carry out his crucifixion: "Father, forgive them; for they know not what they do." His second word is to his fellow sufferer on the cross next to him: "Today you will be with me in Paradise." His third word is to his mother and his disciple John, who stand at the foot of the cross: "Behold your son! Behold your mother!"

The record tells us that for three hours from twelve noon on that day, Jesus endured the darkness of forsakenness. When God became man, he took human form in the womb of a human mother; he lived a normal human life; at the age of thirty, he who had no need to repent took his place alongside repentant sinners and accepted the baptism of repentance for the remission of sins; for three years after that, he carried on his heart and mind the woes and worries of men and women—oppressed by the circumstances of life, his compassion made him one with them; on the cross, he carried the guilt of the sin that crucified him; now at last, he strikes bottom. God not only becomes man, he becomes sinful man. On his lips is the cry of the sinner: "My God, my God, why hast thou forsaken me?" The incarnation is accomplished. Then follow in quick succession the three last words: "I thirst"; "It is finished"; "Father, into thy hands I commit my spirit!"

The Garden Tomb

In the place where Jesus was crucified there was a garden, and in the garden a new sepulcher. Joseph of Arimathea, one of the councillors, comes forward to take charge of the body of Jesus. He obtains permission from Pilate. Nicodemus helps him. They hurriedly embalm the body with a mixture of myrrh and aloes, wrap it in linen cloth, and lay it in the newly hewn tomb. The high priest and the others go to Pilate with a request that the tomb be guarded. They do so, because in all the evidence that night in the palace of Caiaphas, the only bit of clear testimony was to this word of Jesus: "This man said, 'I will destroy this temple that is made with hands, and in three days I will build another made without hands.'" What Caiaphas and the others understood by this we cannot say; but they were certainly anxious. Pilate asks them to see to the matter themselves. They go and seal the tomb and set a guard; and so return home satisfied that their work is done. Jesus will trouble them no more. But . . . .

Ever since that day, this "but" has stared mankind in the face—the "but" of God's triumphant possibility, the "but" of God's reply to man's deed of sin.

Easter Morning—Christus Victor

At this point in the Gospel story, many who attempt to retell the story leave the Gospel records alone and seek to

81

state, as they say, in contemporary speech, the meaning of the
Gospel declaration that Jesus rose from the dead. I cannot
allow myself to do this because I am convinced that the Gospel writers intend the Easter stories as a continuation of the
story that they have been telling. Let us listen to what the
stories themselves say.

Joseph of Arimathea and Nicodemus had taken down the
body of Jesus, wrapped it in its grave clothes, put one hun-
dred pounds of spices within the folds, laid the body inside
the tomb, and rolled the stone against the door of the
sepulcher. The tomb was then sealed (John 19:38-42; Matt.
27:66). At sunset on Saturday the Sabbath was over, but
women could not go out in the darkness of the night. Day-
break on Sunday morning would give them their first opportunity to go to the tomb. So the women who loved Jesus
gather together and, with spices to anoint his body, hurry to
the tomb in the dim light of the early dawn to do for him
what could not be done in a hurried burial. Who will roll
away the stone? It is not impossible to imagine Mary of
Magdala saying, "We shall find a way. I know these men."
But when they get to the tomb, they find the stone rolled
away. The women peep in, and a voice tells them: "He has
risen, he is not here. . . . Go, tell his disciples and Peter"
(Mark 16:1-8).

Mary of Magdala is the first to rush away to bring the
news to the disciples. Peter and John run to the tomb as soon
as they receive Mary's message. Mary follows them. John gets
there first, and stands outside looking through the opening.
Peter arrives and goes right in. John enters with him. And

they find the grave clothes just as they were—the cloth covering the head in its place, the cloth covering the body in its place, and the spices still within the folds. No one has disturbed the cloth; no one could have stolen the body without some of the spices falling on the ground. The truth was obvious: Jesus was not there (John 20:1-10).

Peter and John return to tell their story. But Mary sits outside the tomb weeping. Jesus comes to her and reveals himself to her by the tone in which he calls her. "Mary," he calls, and Mary knows him; for no one else had ever addressed her in exactly that voice. "Do not hold me," he says, "I do not belong any more to you in the flesh. I go to my Father and your Father. I am now Emmanuel for everyone" (see John 20:11-18). Soon after, Jesus appears to the other women also who had come to the tomb, and they bring the news to the disciples that they have seen him (Matt. 28:8-10).

By this time it is long past midday, and two of the disciples set out on their way to their home in Emmaus. They meet with Jesus on the way, but know him not. Jesus explains to them how the prophets had taught that the Christ must suffer and enter into his glory, "and beginning with Moses and all the prophets, he interpreted to them in all the scriptures the things concerning himself." Finally he reveals himself to them in the breaking of bread (Luke 24:13-35).

That same evening Jesus meets Peter (Luke 24:34). The women had delivered the message that they had received: "Go, tell his disciples and Peter." We can imagine Peter going out into that garden, perhaps continuing to sit there after his first visit to the tomb, wondering, wondering, wondering. He had denied his Lord. Would Jesus come to meet him, and if he did, what would he say? Jesus and Peter meet, but what happened at that meeting we do not know. In any case, Peter returned to his brethren, a man the sunshine of whose soul had been washed by rain. When the disciples from Emmaus returned, they said, "We have seen him." The disciples replied, "Yes, he is risen and he has appeared to Simon." While they are still talking, Jesus comes into their midst. "Peace," he says, and there was peace. But Thomas was not there when this happened. We know Thomas, and how, when Jesus left Perea to go to Bethany after the death of Lazarus, he said, "Let us also go and die with him." Thomas had a true assessment of the situation. He was a thinker who knew the implications of believing certain things, the implication of certain things being true. The disciples say to Thomas, "Jesus has risen and we have met him." Thomas refuses to believe. Too much was true if that was true.

We pass quickly from this day to that day when Jesus appeared to Thomas also. But the Gospels tell us that there was a gap of seven days of agony for Thomas. Had he doubted too much? Would he see Jesus? But Jesus appeared again on the next Sunday after Easter, the disciples being gathered together. "Come here, Thomas," he said. "Put your finger into my wounds." Thomas fell down before him and confessed, "My Lord and my God!" (John 20:19-29).

The first disciples saw and believed. We, their children, have not seen but still believe. But that which was given to them is given to us also: to meet Jesus, not indeed in the flesh but yet in the body, person to person. And he gives us the same commission that he gave to those disciples when he met them at the last: "You shall be my witnesses in Jerusalem, that is, at home; in Judea, that is, in the neighborhood; in Samaria, where at first there is no welcome; and unto the uttermost parts of the world."

CHAPTER 4

Our main concern thus far has been to look at the Gospel narratives and their testimony to Jesus Christ. We have noted not only how the Gospels make central the question, "Who is Jesus Christ?" but also tell his story in such a way as to carry conviction concerning his identity. Our attempt now will be to look at the testimony of the whole New Testament, seeking thus to understand how the identity of Jesus Christ informed the total faith of the church and controlled the message which it proclaimed.

I have used the title, "The Finality of Jesus Christ," because I believe that this phrase, more than any other, describes the thrust of the New Testament proclamation: the crux of the issue being that if Jesus is God incarnate, we need to speak of him in the universal terms in which we speak about God, as well as be specific about the particularity that belongs to him as man. The term "unique," as applied to Jesus Christ, which carried the burden of this discussion for many decades, has now been largely abandoned, because its natural context lay in the field of comparative religion, which is a method of studying religions that inevitably leaves the student himself arbiter over the issues involved.

The primary question cannot be what we think of Jesus, but what it is that the New Testament says about him. It is only then that the question arises as to whether we accept this testimony of the New Testament to him or not.

THE
FINALITY
OF
JESUS CHRIST

Many years ago, when my second son was quite a little boy, I took him to the Dalada Maligawa, where the tooth of the Buddha is kept as a relic. It is the most famous Buddhist temple in Ceylon. In one corner of the temple is a huge statue of the Buddha. When I explained to my son who the Buddha was, he said to me, "Yes, and after he died, he would have gone to Jesus Christ. What did Jesus Christ do to him?" When Paul preached to the Athenians on Mars' Hill, his final declaration was, "God . . . has fixed a day when he will judge the world in righteousness by a man whom he has appointed, and of this he has given assurance to all men by raising him from the dead" (Acts 17:31). In the parable of Jesus on the last judgment, it is the Son of man who comes in his glory as the judge (Matt. 25:31 ff.).

The Man Jesus

To speak of the finality of Jesus Christ is to speak specifically of the man Jesus. It is to talk neither about the finality of the Christ-experience, nor about the finality of the Christ-revelation, but about Jesus Christ himself. The issue is not whether all true religious experience is an experience of God in Jesus Christ, nor whether Jesus Christ is the final and, therefore, determinative revelation of God; but whether it is true that God has set, in the world and among men, this man Jesus as final—him to whom they must hearken, him whom they must obey, him through whom they will live and by whom they will be judged. Is Paul right when he says, "For although . . . there are many 'gods' and many 'lords'— yet for us there is one God, the Father, from whom are all things and for whom we exist, and one Lord, Jesus Christ, through whom are all things and through whom we exist"? (I Cor. 8:5-6.)

Some time ago, at an international student conference of theological students, I had a strange experience. I found myself listening to a discussion about Jesus Christ, only to find that the Jesus Christ they were talking about was simply a historical point of reference around whom a body of doctrine and ethics had been built. They kept on saying, this is the Jesus Christ whom through the centuries the church has believed in and proclaimed and whom Christians have experienced. But they denied that it was possible really to know what Jesus Christ was like or said or did when he walked the earth in the flesh. There was a bare skeleton of events which could be attested to with certainty. The rest was claimed to be "proclamation." It is not my intention to go into this question at this time. But I do want to say that, if our attempt thus far to get within hearing and seeing distance of the man Jesus has been a failure, then talk about the finality of Jesus Christ is simply futile. The crux of the finality issue is whether or not in Jesus Christ men confront and are confronted by the transcendent God whose will they cannot manipulate, by whose judgment they are bound, and with whose intractable presence in their midst they must reckon.

The Coordinates of Faith—the Universal and the Particular

As one lives and works with men of other faiths, one is made constantly aware not only of the fact that Christians have beliefs different from those who are not Christian, but also of the fact that they believe in a different way. The very act of faith is different. The basic reason for this is that the coordinates within which the graph of the Christian faith is plotted are quite different from the coordinates used in other religions and other systems of belief. It is not simply that the graphs themselves are different.

One basic difference is that whereas, in all other religions, the coordinates of faith are determined by the relation between the infinite and the finite, the eternal and the temporal, in Christianity they are determined by the relation between the universal and the particular. The scriptural testimony is not that Jesus Christ is a finite manifestation of the infinite, but that he is the universal become particular—the image of the invisible God (Col. 1:15). Jesus Christ is neither a darshana nor an avatar.

The point at issue is the difference between the various experiences of meeting God and the experience of the compulsive specific obedience which one has when one meets Jesus. Jesus of Nazareth, whenever he addressed men, addressed them with specific demands: leave your nets, take up your bed, sell what you have. He is still the same Jesus. The experience of meeting God which is known as the mystical experience, and which is testified to by the devotees in all religions, is best understood within the relation between the infinite and the finite. When one is talking about the finality of Jesus Christ, however, one is talking about how this mystical experience is pegged down to this earthly life. To paraphrase Paul, the particular consists "in the works he has prepared for us to walk in" (Eph. 2:10).

That which is being contended for is not the prestige of a particular place of meeting between God and man, but the peculiarity of what happens when men meet God in Jesus Christ. When Jesus announced that "the kingdom of God is at hand," and demanded of men that they "repent, and believe in the gospel" (Mark 1:15), he was asking not for some general response to the requirements of religion or morality, but for a specific commitment to a particular event and person. The religious man is one kind of man, a Christian disciple is another kind of man. There is no substitute for the "shattering" which takes place when men meet God at God's place and hour of appointment, and for the consequences in discipline and discipleship of that experience.

Attempts have been made, again and again, to change this axis around which the Christian faith rotates, to change these coordinates within which the graph of that faith is plotted. There have always been those who have desired to understand the Christian faith, not in terms of the relation between the universal and the particular, but in terms of the relation between the infinite and the finite, the eternal and the temporal. In this discussion, the crux of the argument has always been concerning the resurrection of Jesus Christ. The New Testament insistence on the decisive significance of the resurrection of Jesus Christ constitutes a denial of the view that Jesus is a temporal manifestation of the eternal God, a finite appearance of him who is infinite. The finite and the temporal are categories which apply to that which is repeatable. The resurrection faith, however, is concerned with the eternity and universality of Jesus Christ himself. What the New Testament is announcing is not that the Christ-experience cannot be destroyed by death, nor that in the Christ-revelation death is seen to be not final, but that Jesus himself rose from the dead. The testimony is not to the life of Jesus after death, but to his conquest of death. What the New Testament makes clear is that while the risen Christ offers himself only to the perception of faith, he is nevertheless to be proclaimed to all men as having risen from the dead. There is a happening apart from faith which is proclaimed, even though it is to faith that the proclamation is addressed. As Paul puts it, "God . . . has given assurance to all men by raising him from the dead" (Acts 17:31). When Peter says, "This Jesus, . . . you crucified and killed. . . . But God raised him up" (Acts 2:23-24), he means not something that had happened to the disciples, but something that had happened to Jesus.

Also, even as by its testimony to the resurrection of Jesus Christ the New Testament witnesses to the eternity of the specific man Jesus, even so by its testimony to the ascension of Jesus Christ the New Testament seeks to say that in Jesus the distinction between the infinite and the finite is an irrelevant distinction. "Seated at the right hand of God" is a way of saying that here is the operative reality, the whole is present at this point and in this person, this is both the infinite and the finite, he is what God is with respect to all things—their Sovereign and Savior, their Judgment and their Judge.

Now we can see how it is that, while the New Testament testimony is to a specific event which happened, it is able also to speak of this event in the present tense. For precisely in the fact that the New Testament faith concerning Jesus Christ is stated unambiguously in terms of the relation between the universal and the particular lies the ground for the New Testament witness that Jesus Christ is the same yesterday, today, and forever (Heb. 13:8). The finality that is asserted is not the finality of an event in the past or a person in the past, but the finality of him who is continuously and identifiably present. "He must reign until he has put all his enemies under his feet." (I Cor. 15:25.) "I am with you always, to the close of the age." (Matt. 28:20.)

When God revealed himself to Moses, he revealed himself

as one who was recognized by being continuously present, and by being known by that presence alone (Exod. 3:14). Moses had to lead his people to follow a God who would never become past tense. The second commandment, "You shall not make yourself a graven image" (Exod. 20:4), is a commandment not to attempt to make God static. Indeed, no understanding of God which is delimited by a past tense is satisfactory. The attraction of thinking in terms of the infinite and the finite is that the finite can keep on repeating itself so that no past tense need be determinative. There is no finality because there is constant repetition. As the Bhagavad Gita has it, "Though unborn and immutable in essence, though Lord of Beings, yet governing Nature which is mine, I come into being by my delusive power. For whensover right declines, O Bharata, and wrong uprises, then I create myself" (iv. 6-7).

The biblical faith has a different thrust. The finality which is affirmed about Jesus Christ is set within the context of an ongoing activity of God, whereby the past does not remain past but is continuously becoming present. In the Exodus passage to which reference has been made, it is the God of Abraham, Isaac, and Jacob who reveals himself to Moses as "I am." So also, the New Testament witness to the finality of Jesus Christ is not simply to the finality of a past event, but of a present Savior. It is the same bush which is burning without being consumed. When the church confesses, "And I believe in Jesus Christ—born, suffered, crucified, died, and buried; who rose again and has ascended and will come," it is of the same Jesus that every item in this confession is made (Acts 1:11). It is he who is final; not that everything is over, but that he encompasses everything that takes place. In the closing words of the Bible, as Jesus speaks them, "I am the Alpha and the Omega, the first and the last, the beginning and the end" (Rev. 22:13).

The Coordinates of Faith—This World and This Life

This way of relating past tense to present tense takes the discussion from a consideration of the person of Christ to a consideration of his work. When Jesus declared that the kingdom of God had come, there was a double thrust in that declaration. The event of the coming was past tense. But the kingdom of God itself was present continuous tense. The finality of Jesus Christ is the finality of an ongoing work.

This indissoluble connection between the person of Jesus Christ and his work, when speaking of his finality, leads to a clarification of a second basis of difference between the co-ordinates of the Christian faith and those of other faiths and beliefs. The scriptures of other religions deal fundamentally either with the interior life or the life after death. The Christian scriptures, however, speak in the first instance about this present life in this world in all its concreteness and its particularities. Other religions hold that the important thing in the drama of life is what happens to the actors; while the Christian scriptures affirm that what happens to the actors is only a part of God's concern. His total concern encompasses the whole drama—men, women, and children, and all of nature, in their relationships to one another and in their several particularities of age and sex, of community and race, of nation and religion, and across the generations of time. It is this insistence on this world and this life which gives to the New Testament declaration that in Jesus God became man its true context.

When the name of Jesus is announced as "Emmanuel"—"God with us" (Matt. 1:23), the announcement affirms the "with-ness" of God on which human life depends. Man is made in the image of God (Gen. 1:27). This imaging relationship, in which man is perpetually placed before God, constitutes the meaning and responsibility of human life. The God-man relationship is a treble one. "In him we live and move and have our being." (Acts 17:28.) But this God, in whom we are, is also the God who is within us (Col. 1:27). He is constantly in our lives and within our personalities seeking to evoke in us a true response to himself. In the third place, he to whom this response has to be made, and who is seeking this response, is also constantly present as the reality of God outside us, impinging on us, both in wrath and in mercy, both in judgment and in demand (Rev. 3:20). There is no way of simplifying the God-man relationship so that any one of these three relations—God's inclusiveness, his immanence, and his transcendence—is subsumed under the other two. When Scripture testifies to the finality of Jesus Christ, it is speaking of this fact of Jesus as Emmanuel, God with us, in the richness of this threefold relation, and in so doing, bears witness to the several aspects of the work of Christ.

1. The first strand in the biblical testimony to the work of Jesus Christ is that it is *he from whom all things proceed and receive their vocation.* Paul states this quite directly when he says, "All things were created through him and for him"

(Col. 1:16). Scripture does not find it a logical burden to attribute to Jesus Christ the origin of things, because it sees clearly that their meaning is in him. All things were not only made through him, but nothing made is outside him (John 1:13). He is the one in whom all things are, and who is in all things. Their true nature and vocation is what he is in them and what they are in him.

The significance of what is being said here lies in the fact that, by this way of saying it, the Creator and his creation are shown as being bound together. "He through whom all things were created is also the first-born of all creation." (See Col. 1:15-16.) The whole of creation is invested with meaning because he is part of them. In him the "with-ness" of God is affirmed. All things are from him and he is of them.

2. The natural next step in the biblical testimony is to speak of Jesus Christ as *he in whom all things cohere and work together* (Col. 1:17). Everything keeps moving and changing, and yet the whole thing holds together. Things do not fly apart. Life remains a unity in spite of all its diversity. The mystery of evil too is held within the exercise of God's sovereign grace (II Thess. 2:7-8). An inclusive purpose binds everything together, a purpose which belongs to someone in ultimate authority. Men experience this ultimacy in personal life, as they see how he rules and overrules all things, "in everything [working] for good with all those who love him" (Rom. 8:28); while, in the life of society, this ultimacy is maintained and declared through a mission. "All authority in heaven and on earth," Jesus says, "has been given to me. Go therefore and make disciples of all nations" (Matt. 28:18-19). The apostles are sent everywhere and to

everyone, because everywhere and over everyone, Jesus is already in authority. No wonder Paul in his close-knit argument in his letter to the Romans makes Jesus Christ the key to the understanding of the whole of history. "No failure," he says, "is final. No betrayal or disobedience is ultimate. There is always a way out of what seems a blind alley. No one is outside the overarching purposes of God. O the depth of the riches and wisdom and knowledge of God! How unsearchable are his judgments, and how inscrutable his ways! For from him and through him and to him are all things." (Rom. 11: 33, 36.)

This way of stating the finality of Jesus rests on the fact that, as he is part of creation and is himself involved in human history, that which happened to him must become the source of that which happens to all. He is the pioneer of our salvation (Heb. 2:10). So that even as it is possible to speak of the whole as being infected by sin, we can speak of the whole as being infected by salvation (I Cor. 15:21-22). The pioneer does not set an example to be followed; he opens up a highway by which men can now go to the land that has been won for them by him.

3. However, the teaching of Scripture is not that in Jesus all is now well, and well anyhow. Jesus is *he by whom all things are judged and brought to judgment*. His finality bears a consequence for all things.

As John puts it, the fact that God has sent his Son into the world sets before men a real choice—either to believe in him and so to share in eternal life, the life which he lives in the world; or to live apart from him and so to perish (John 3:16). That which has perished has no use. Just as a fruit which has perished is useless for eating, so he who has perished is of no use to Jesus Christ. And, conversely, to be of no use to Jesus Christ is to perish.

The point is that there is a determining reality in the world which is Jesus Christ at work in it. "In him was life, and the life was the light of men." (John 1:4.) This light has now come into the world (John 1:9). So that the life he lives in the world becomes the way by which all men must walk, as it also decides the way in which all men must work. As he himself explained it, only those who work with him gather, while the rest only scatter (Luke 11:23).

4. But this testimony to the activity of God in judgment, of which Jesus Christ is the judge because he is God's intervention in and God's decision for human life, is set within the context of the promise that Jesus is *he through whom all things fulfill their destiny*.

In the prophecy of Jeremiah, the new beginning is set out in these terms: "I will put my law within them, and I will write it upon their hearts; . . . for I will forgive their iniquity, and I will remember their sin no more" (Jer. 31:33-34). A great act of forgiveness is the matrix within which judgment is exercised; or, in New Testament terms, Christ's act of atonement is also the basis of the judgment he exercises.

The New Testament does not worry about the logical contradiction between its teaching that damnation is a possibility for men, so that this may be the judgment which is pronounced on some at the last, and its teaching that God's plan in Christ for the fullness of time is to unite all things in him (Eph. 1:10). Indeed, the New Testament shows that it is out of this very contradiction that there arises both the gospel which is proclaimed and the reason for proclaiming it. If salvation is by grace, damnation cannot be by works; so that the issue of faith and unfaith must be stringently understood in relation to the person and work of Jesus Christ.

This recapitulation, however, of all things in Jesus Christ at the end of the process of history is already taking place in the world. It is personal experience that when the entries in the book of men's lives are brought under the heading of Jesus Christ, many a transaction which seemed at the time to be gain will be seen really to have been loss, while others which seemed at the time to have been loss will be seen to be gain. Besides, because this life and activity of Jesus Christ is his life and activity in the world, it is meaningful to speak too of human cultures beng recapitulated in him and through him. Thus, when an Indian thinker speaks of "wedding the Spirit of Christ with the spirit of India," he is asking that Christ's presence in India be discerned so that that which belongs to India may be brought into his obedience and into the service of his glory. "They shall bring into [Zion] the glory and the honor of the nations." (Rev. 21:26.)

5. The climax of the biblical testimony, therefore, to the finality of Jesus Christ is that it is *he unto whom all things go.* This is the natural climax to the affirmation that the finality of Jesus Christ is not simply the finality of himself as a person, but is also the finality of his work as the effective presence in the world of the kingdom and reign of God.

On the one hand, there is this reign as it impinges on human life through the exercise of Christ's Lordship and Saviorhood. On the other hand, there is the work of the Holy Spirit in the hearts and minds of men, evoking repentance and faith, and enabling the response of obedience and discipleship. The finality of Jesus Christ receives its full Trinitarian affirmation only as it takes seriously this New Testament witness to the work of the Holy Spirit. For apart from him, the gift of grace in Jesus Christ is not received. It is the Holy Spirit who teaches men to live by the Father's welcome, enabling each man to say, "Abba! Father!" It is also by him that they are led to inherit that which Jesus Christ has made their inheritance (Rom. 8:16-17).

This essential work of the Holy Spirit has as its hallmark the way in which things and persons are brought to participation in the crisis of Christ's death and resurrection. Individuals die with him in his death, and find that in losing themselves they save themselves. Also, every perception of truth and every system of moral behavior is brought to dissolution by him, when it is submitted to him, and then resurrected to new life within his obedience and in his service.

The Coordinates of Faith—the Eschatological Community and Its Witness

The finality of Jesus Christ, as the Bible declares it, however, does not consist only in the finality of the Person and his work. It also consists in the finality of the witness borne to him. The community which carries his name bears this finality as a mark of its life.

When Scripture works out the relation between the universal and the particular in the structure of Christian faith, it also includes in its teaching the way in which this relation is exemplified in the reality of the church—that is, in the relation between the purposes of God for the whole of creation and the work of God in the community of witness. This is why the Christian community is compared to the first fruits of a harvest. The first fruits are the guarantee of the whole harvest and part of it. As James has it, "Of his own will he brought us forth by the word of truth that we should be a kind of first fruits of his creatures" (James 1:18). The call and the blessing of Abraham, which is the first act in the story of how the whole human community took particular form in a people bearing God's name, has this relation between the universal and the particular explicitly stated in the call itself. "I will bless you . . . and by you all the families of the earth will bless themselves." (Gen. 12:2-3.)

How does this happen? The answer given is to speak of the representative nature of Christ as well as to speak of the way in which the church participates in that nature. In his letter to the Hebrews the writer says, "As it is we do not yet see everything in subjection to him. But we see Jesus" (Heb. 2:8-9). The thrust of the verse is not that that which is not yet will be accomplished because of what has already happened in and to Jesus Christ, but that what has happened in and to Jesus Christ is already the end, the end toward which all things are set. "We grow," says Paul, "into him who is the head, into Christ" (Eph. 4:15).

Jesus Christ is representative man. That which happened to him happened to all humanity, so that it is this happening which is then unfolded through the process of time. The passage in Daniel (Dan. 7:13-14), to which the verse in Hebrews alludes, speaks of the Son of man. The Son of man is man in his divine human-ness. He is what God intended man to be. When Jesus chose this title for himself (Matt. 16:13), this was the claim that he was making. "I am man." And, when his disciples called him the Son of God (Matt. 16:16), that was their way of accepting his claim. For the Son of man is Son of man only because he is the Son of God. He is God's decisive deed on man's behalf. He is for man his new beginning. In him all humanity is represented.

Also, since there is only one name by which men can be saved (Acts 4:12), only one way to the Father (John 14:6), therefore in him all must meet. If there are many ways for men to attain their destiny, they can go by those several ways without meeting one another. But if there is only one way and one door, all men must meet. The human community is constituted by the finality of Jesus Christ. All things are not only from him, but unto him.

In this representativeness of Christ the church shares because, not only are all things set toward him, but he himself who is the end has happened to the church. In Paul's words, the church is that on which the "end of the ages has come" (I Cor. 10:11). It is that for which tomorrow is over. It is the eschatological community. In describing the Christian life, both John and Paul use violent metaphors. John speaks of a second birth (John 3:3), while Paul speaks of a death and resurrection (Rom. 6:3-4). There is one thing certain about every child when it is born—it will die. Paul makes the claim that, for the Christian, this certain event is over. He has already died. The death he will die some day is only the physical counterpart of a death he has died already. That is why death has no sting and the grave no victory (I Cor. 15:55). The life of the church is this resurrected life. "Destroy this temple," Jesus said, "and . . . I will raise it up" (John 2:19). John adds the comment, "He spoke of the temple of his body" (John 2:21).

How many Christians live as those for whom death is over? What will it mean to do so? It will mean, will it not, that when they do something well they will be able to forget it and not be disappointed if no one gives them credit for it. They will know what it is to have the signature of death written across all their achievements, just as it has been written across all their sins. How many (and here I am talking about Ceylon) profess that they are prepared to carry the cross for Jesus' sake, but decide to emigrate if they are overlooked for a promotion on the ground that they are Christians! No, it cannot be said of most of us that we are dead. We are very much alive to what we think the world owes us. The Christian practice of death means nothing more and nothing less than allowing people to treat us as they treated Jesus himself. When Paul said, "I am dead, but Christ is alive in me" (see Gal. 2:20), he was saying, "You can deal with me as you dealt with Jesus Christ." That is the crux of the Christian calling. "Are you able," Jesus asks, "to drink the cup that I drink, or to be baptized with the baptism with which I am baptized?" (Mark 10:38.)

The other side of this truth is that not only is death over but the resurrection is over too. He who is risen is already the Lord. And yet, how little acknowledgment is made of this lordship. There is too great a readiness to harbor grievances, to press claims, to ask for recognition, as if the final reality is not the lordship of Christ but the freedom of men. It is true, is it not, that as far as any man is concerned, he is not at another man's mercy, not even his own, for Christ is already Lord of all men and all things.

But it is not only in this personal dimension that witness is borne to the finality of Christ; for, if Christ is final, witness concerning him must be borne to others also. This means the acceptance of the fact of the presence of Jesus Christ in the history of all other faiths, as well as the acceptance of the responsibility to declare to men of other faiths the identity of the "unknown God" by whom each man's faith is validated and their systems of faith are judged (Acts 17:23).

To disclose the "unknown God" is not to rename the known gods. Instead, it is to uncover a presence which has been there even though unidentified; indeed, a presence that was forgotten and lost, if not denied. To put this matter in another way, the known gods represent the past tense in one's religious history. It is the present tense, the way in which God is contemporarily present, which needs to be discerned and named. That this present tense has always been present is what makes the name of Jesus appropriate for it.

The naming of the "unknown God" rests too on another fact: that when Jesus Christ makes his place and time of appointment with men, he does not always give his name. I can imagine a man like Jawaharlal Nehru saying, "But when did I see you naked or hungry or in prison?" (Matt. 25:37-39). The point is not that there are alternatives to commitment to Christ—other ways by which men can be saved—but that to speak about the finality of Christ is not to tie oneself to where his name is actually pronounced. As he himself tells us, he determines the form and occasion of his presence, and where and to whom he will come incognito.

Also, is it not the converse of this fact that he is emphasizing when he says that if the son who has said "Yes" will not obey, then the father will win his obedience from the son who says "No" (Matt. 21:28-31)?

To fulfill, then, the Christian responsibility with regard to other faiths and their adherents, Christians must, as it were, be prepared to engage simultaneously in three dialogues. First, there will be the inner dialogue through which their own faith in Jesus Christ is matured and fructified by the testimony of other men to God's ways with them. The Christian must never forget that he is always as one who sees baffling reflections in a mirror (I Cor. 13:12), and that others constantly make clear to him things which he finds perplexing. Secondly, there will be the outer dialogue in which Christians and those who are not engage each other in conversation. The intent of this dialogue is to discern the ways of God in each other's religion and religious experience—in the questions that are asked, the search which is conducted, and the answers found. For nowhere has God left himself without witness (Acts 14:17). Also, since the Holy Spirit is at work in the lives of all men, each man is at a particular moment in Jesus Christ. It is this moment, with respect to each, which needs to be discerned so that the dialogue may take place in the company of Jesus. And finally, there is the essential dialogue between each man and Jesus Christ in which, as it were, those in outer dialogue stand by one another silently, upholding one another in mutual concern. The culmination of this essential dialogue for all men has to be their conversion to Jesus Christ—him with whom they must die and by and for whom they must live. The witness of the Christian to the finality of Jesus Christ is a witness through and within all these three dialogues.

But Christian witness to the finality of Jesus Christ has a third implication also; for there is the witness to be borne together by those who bear his name. The issues concerning church union have their own inherent difficulty. This is no place to talk about them. Nevertheless, it is essential to remember here that no one may talk about the finality of Christ and, at the same time, remain careless of the necessity of all those who bear his name belonging to one family and living a common family life. Jesus Christ must be sufficient for his people, both to unite them and to enable them to be enriched by their differences. The tragedy of denominations is that they are an attempt to organize dogmatic differences, to give to the baffling reflections institutional and structural expression. The finality of Jesus Christ is a standing judgment on denominational separateness. He alone is enough.

The church cannot fulfill its role as the home of the human dialogue, the dialogue between man and man and between man and God, if it does not in its own life sustain that dialogue. It is the foundation of the church which is fixed; its walls on every side must have open gates through which the traffic of life can flow. To close these gates against fellow Christian or fellowman is to deny the nature of the church.

We have referred already to two basic differences in the structure of faith between Christianity and other religions. We have seen that the coordinates within which the graph of the Christian faith was plotted were determined by the relation between the universal and the particular as that relation is in Jesus Christ, and also by the this-worldliness which the coming of Jesus Christ signifies, and to which it gives effect. We can state now the third factor which constitutes this difference: that whereas, in all other religions and systems of belief, the present is determined by the past, in Christianity the present is determined by the future. It is to this difference that the Christian community bears witness by the eschatological nature of its existence, the implications of which are what we have been discussing.

An integral part of the good news of the gospel is in this fact that the future is over, and that the history of man is not something that is being pushed from behind but is something that is being pulled from in front. Indeed, this witness to an accomplished future toward which all things are set is part of the biblical testimony to the transcendence of God. Here is the reason for that intractability and intransigence with which men find they have to deal, both in their personal lives and behavior and in their life together as communities. Whenever Scripture speaks about predestination, it is about the destination that it speaks. It is the destination which has been determined.

To believe that today is determined by yesterday is to believe in salvation by works; whereas, to believe that today is determined by tomorrow is to believe in salvation by grace. Yesterday is over, yes; but tomorrow is over too. He who will be crowned Lord is Lord already. He who will come to judge is already engaged in judgment. The final consummation is already the end toward which all things are set. The fruits of men's labor are already the gifts of his love.

> Jesus knowing that . . . he had come from God and was going to God . . . girded himself with a towel. (John 13:3-4.)

CHAPTER 5

Does the Bible simply contain a collection of miscellaneous Christologies and ecclesiologies, or does the biblical message have a substantial unity? On the answer to this question depends the very foundation of the church's calling. In the way in which we have dealt with the biblical testimony, we have assumed the cohesion and unity of that testimony, and trusted the result of our study itself to show that this cohesion and unity actually exist.

The unity of the biblical message is founded on the common faith of the biblical writers that the true meaning of events lies in their place within the divine activity; and that it is this activity in creation and redemption, judgment and mercy, selection and rejection, destruction and fulfillment which is also the subject of the divine disclosure. Of this disclosure, the Christ-event is the consummation.

This event—its nature, meaning, consequences, and challenge— is our subject. But, whereas thus far we have stayed within the confines of the biblical testimony, it is now our intention to face up to the implications of that testimony as we listen to it from the actual world in which we live. To put it in another way, the question about Jesus Christ is not, in the last analysis, a question we ask about him, but a question which he asks us about himself. It is his question: Who do you say that I am?

WHO
DO
YOU SAY
THAT I AM?

When Jesus asks me, "Who am I?" I know that it is not enough for me simply to say, "You are the Christ of God." I know that that answer will remain empty of meaning until it is stated and restated in terms of the actual challenges amidst which I live, until it is clothed with the world from which I come. The answer must become contemporary.

We come to the experience of Jesus as our contemporary by a double movement. There is first of all the simple fact that he comes to us and meets us along life's road—not some memory of him but he himself, the risen Lord. As the well-known children's hymn has it,

Who Is This Jesus?

Wise men seeking Jesus travelled from afar
Guided on their journey by a beauteous star.
But if we desire Him, He is close at hand;
For our native country is our Holy Land.

And then there is the invitation which the Gospel records bring, that we go to meet him in the days of his flesh and encounter him in the world in which he lived among his contemporaries of that day. This is what we have tried to do as we allowed ourselves to listen to the Gospel story. As we have seen, that story is told in such a way that those who listen find themselves involved in the events which take place, challenged by the controversies these events aroused, and under pressure to answer the one question which every story and incident hammers out: "Who do you say that I am?"

In the confession which I make as to who Jesus is, it must somehow both be true that I answer him because he has come to me and met me in my world, and that I have gone to him and met him in his. To put it in another way, it is not the meaning of Jesus Christ which must be stated in contemporary terms; Jesus himself, in his concreteness, must be seen as contemporary.

Why use the word "concreteness"? Because some aspects of New Testament scholarship seem to be intended so to analyze what has gone into the making of the Gospels that, after the analysis, it is impossible to put the parts together again. To use a figure, the Gospels are like a beautiful chain made by consummate craftsmen, who have hung on that chain four beautiful pendants. Each pendant has a gem within it, set within exquisite workmanship. It is possible to break the chain, to take the pendants apart. It is possible to destroy the pendants and pry the gems loose. But when this has been done, the way in which the chain and the pendants have been dismembered makes it impossible to put them back together again. Some scholars even give the impression that they are so suspicious of the gems that they would rather find a way independent of the gems for preserving the light in them. The result is that one is left with an "Alice in Wonderland" effect, where the grin remains while the cat has disappeared.

And so (and I repeat myself again), it is not the meaning of Jesus Christ which must be stated in contemporary terms; Jesus himself, in his concreteness, must be seen as contemporary.

In Buddhism and Islam, religions which have founders, the claim that is made for the founder is that he taught the truth. His teaching carries him. In the case of Jesus, he carries his teaching. Indeed, it is said quite explicitly not only that he himself is the truth (John 14:6), but that his teaching is not a complete exposition of that truth. As John has it, Jesus said to his disciples, "I have yet many things to say to you, but you cannot bear them now. When the Spirit of truth comes, he will guide you into all the truth; . . . for he will take what is mine and declare it to you" (John 16:12-15).

It will be found that as I proceed with this discussion, the background against which the discussion is conducted is not merely that of the religions amidst which I live, but also of the echoes of contemporary theological debate as they reach my part of the world from the West where these debates are largely conducted. For even though in the West these debates are debates between Christian thinkers, for us the echoes

111

of them are reminiscent of debates of long ago, as they were conducted within our ancient religions and between them.

It is perhaps necessary to say one thing more at this point, and that is to confess to the perplexities which much of the theological debate in the West has given rise to among those who are the rank and file of church members, whether in East or West. My concern is largely with these perplexities. I do not intend either to name names or to discuss the exact teaching of any particular school of thought. I do not possess the refinements of scholarships which such a discussion will need, nor am I really keen to enter into such a discussion. I am much more alive to the perplexities, as I have called them, in which Christians find themselves, because they find it so hard to see how the New Testament and its testimony make sense, should the things that are being said be true. It can be conceded that one must not just read the headlines, but must read also the actual reports. However, the headlines too are important and those whose writings appear under these headlines cannot altogether disclaim them.

The headlines say that God is dead; that it does not make sense to talk about Jesus as God become man; that the Bible can still make sense when God and prayer to him have been abolished; when only categories which relate to man are used to explain Jesus, and when psychology and sociology provide sufficient categories to explain the sinner's sense of guilt or the responsibility of men for one another; that, in any case, what we have in the Bible is a collection of human records of religious or ethical experiences and a miscellaneous attempt to explain these experiences—in other words, that the Bible has neither unity of structure nor message; that Jesus himself

is unknown and unknowable, and that it is not even necessary to know him as he actually lived and worked and taught;
and that the Christian community as an identifiable community has no usefulness or justification anymore. Even if I
am only partially right in saying that these are the headlines,
should we be surprised that in a world in which many read
only the headlines, there is such utter confusion! It is this
world, no less than the world of ancient religions in which I
live, that determines for me the challenges under which I
must give my own answer to the question which I can hear
Jesus asking me: "Who do you say that I am?"

Buddhism

The vast majority of my countrymen are Buddhists. Prince
Siddhartha, who became the Buddha (the Enlightened One),
is for them the man among men. He, above all men, they
claim, understood and explained the meaning of life. So they
seek to spread and to follow his teaching. He taught men to
meet life as an enemy is met and to conquer it, to rise above
its storm and passion, and so to live in recollected peace and
poise so that the bondage of desire is broken. Thus can man
be set free from the succession of many births and deaths in
which this life is involved. The commonest sight in Ceylon
is the picture of the statue of the Buddha—his eyes closed
to the world without, his head erect, the smile of the con-
queror upon his lips, his whole attitude the attitude of one
for whom life has no problems. He is the Buddha, the one
who knows, the one who is wise. How often, when I have
just passed such a statue of the Buddha and seen the people

at their devotions, and then come suddenly upon a Christian church with its cross upon the roof, have I not pondered the question: Which is the true Son of man? Is it he who conquered life or he who conquered death? Is it he who passed beyond pain or he who healed it? Is it the stately Buddha at rest in himself, or that man from Nazareth who had nowhere to lay his head until he laid it on a cross? The contrast between the two figures shouts the question at you: Which is the true response to life—the peace that stands above all desire, or the sorrow of sorrow shared? "Who do you say that I am?" asks Jesus; and the question becomes a challenge in front of every Buddhist shrine.

As has already been mentioned, one of the common catchwords in theological debate today is the statement, "God is dead." Whenever I hear this or read about it, I cannot help but remember that five centuries before Jesus Christ, the Buddha declared that God was dead. Belief in God, in the Hinduism of his day, had either diffused itself into belief in the cosmic soul or made itself cheap in a belief in a multiplicity of gods who could be approached to grant human benefits, but were quite irrelevant in man's struggle and search to find the meaning and purpose of his life. The Buddha brushed aside this belief in God and gods, telling men that they themselves were masters of their own destiny.

In our contemporary theological scene, the announcement that God is dead is followed by an invitation to find life's meaning by following one of three paths, indeed even by following all three paths simultaneously. Let us not worry about God, we are told, but let us concentrate on Jesus Christ; we can find in him the answers to the questions as to what life

is all about. Others tell us that the way to live is for us ourselves to make life meaningful, not that the meaning is in the
meaning made, but in the decision to make meaning; while
still others speak of life's meaning being found by the simple
process of living it. Life, they say, will disclose its own meaning.

It is obvious that the problem which is being attacked is
one that has been caused by the attempt to flatten life out.
Life has ceased to have a horizon and, therefore, the necessity arises to find perspective in some other way. Irrespective
of whether it is true or false that God is dead, and whatever
that means, let us look at the contrast in the testimony to
Jesus Christ between the "God is dead" position and that of
the New Testament. One example will make the point. At
the heart of the biblical testimony to Jesus Christ is the assertion that in him there is a new beginning for all of life.
Paul says, "If any one is in Christ, he is a new creation" (II
Cor. 5:17). The writer to the Hebrews speaks explicitly
when he says, "He abolishes the first in order to establish the
second" (Heb. 10:9). The letter to the Ephesians speaks of
the "new nature, created after the likeness of God" (Eph.
4:24), which nature is Jesus Christ. That is why Paul speaks
about "putting on Jesus Christ" (Rom. 13:14). John declares
that "God sent the Son into the world, not to condemn the
world, but that the world might be saved through him" (John
3:17). Because of Jesus Christ, there is now a new possibility.

The crux of this way of speaking is that Jesus Christ is
related directly to God and, therefore, to the origin of all
things; so that it makes sense to speak of him in terms of a
new beginning, a new origin, of which he is both the source

and the first manifestation. I cannot see how it is possible to take out this reference to God in the total testimony, without that testimony collapsing completely. And when this happens, the result is that the meaning of Jesus has to be the meaning we find in him. Each man can then give his own answer to the question: "Who do you say that I am?" and all answers will be right. What I am struggling to say is something like this: if God is dead, then Jesus cannot be the center of the picture. The center of each man's picture has to be himself, while the center of the total picture has to be man clothed in his own sovereignty. This is what Buddhism does and what the Buddha is.

In fact, the way in which the Buddha dealt with the consequences of saying that God is dead is more radical than the ways which are offered to us by the "God is dead" theologians. The Buddha looked at life and said, If men are to live wisely, they must face three facts. All of these are consequences of a godless world: human personality has no identity, nothing has any permanence, and every aspect of life is not only riddled by the experience of sorrow but determined by it. Man's search for meaning has, therefore, ultimately to be a search for freedom from life itself. This freedom, however, comes to men not as something which they find, but as something which finds them—Nirvana is not object but subject—and the Buddhist way of life is to allow Nirvana to determine that way. The negative which is part of the definition and description of Nirvana must order the way in which man lives and regulate the stages along that way.

Am I wrong in thinking that if it is true that God is dead,

it were better that we became Buddhists and followed the teachings of him who not only said that God was dead long before our modern theologians, but dealt with the consequences of such an affirmation with greater thoroughness and surer consistency? If God is dead, the figure of Jesus Christ does not and cannot make sense, at least not the figure of Jesus Christ as we find him in the records. It is the figure of the Buddha which makes sense in this situation. To the question of Jesus, "Who do you say that I am?" we cannot answer, "You are the one I cling to, you are my Lord, because God is dead." If God is dead, there is no point in clinging to Jesus Christ.

Islam

Islam is a religion in which, if you take away God as the transcendent one, its whole edifice of faith and practice breaks down. Stated in doctrinal terms, Jesus Christ is the incarnation of God. So Christians believe. But to the Muslims, this belief is blasphemy. God is God, and man is man, and Jesus was man. He was a prophet illumined by God's Spirit and entrusted with God's word, but he was only a prophet. Nor was he the greatest of them, for Mohammed was later and greater. It is Mohammed, the Muslim claims, who has brought God's final revelation of himself and his demands; who has established on earth the most inclusive brotherhood of man; and who has set out the law by which man's life is to be governed. The task of the Christian preacher, in the face of Islam, is the task of speaking convincingly about God's method of graciously entering into the human situation and sharing in it; and of showing that God's mercy is available for man not only as revealed word but also as saving presence, not only as law to be obeyed but also as freedom from the law to be enjoyed, not only as the brotherhood of those who believe but also as the community of those who have been forgiven. It is the nature of God as Savior which is under discussion when Jesus is proclaimed to the Muslim as the Son of God. It is difficult to lead the Buddhist to the cross to see there the Son of man; it is difficult to lead the Muslim to the stable at Bethlehem to see there the Son of God. Morning, noon, and night, from every Muslim minaret goes out the cry: "God is great and Mohammed is his prophet." While, matched against that cry, is the question of the child at Bethlehem: "Who do you say that I am?" The question becomes a puzzle in front of every Muslim mosque.

When I come to the West, one of the endemic questions I meet wherever I go is whether morality has any transcendental reference. I never realized the length to which this discussion has gone until at a seminar in which I participated, a young Canadian propounded the thesis that a Christian can also be a prostitute. He said that he had a friend who was a pastor in France who told him that the best Christian in his congregation earned her living by this means. If a prostitute can be a Christian, was the argument, why cannot a Christian be a prostitute? I give this illustration to show that, in its extreme form, situational ethics can lead into a moral forest in which there are no beaten tracks. The problem is not met by saying that even in this new morality there is retained the concept of guilt. The question is whether this sense of guilt has any relation to the offer of forgiveness in Jesus Christ.

Again and again, in discussions, the point is made that it is wrong and unhelpful to apply so-called absolute standards in order to determine, in specific situations, what is the right thing to do. In spite of the validity of this position, the truth that it misses is that forgiveness of sin as it is experienced in Jesus Christ is itself an absolute. A situational ethic which robs Calvary of its meaning has to be thereby condemned. At the meeting of the International Missionary Council held at Tambaram in 1938, Dr. Walter Horton said in one of the discussions, "I live by faith in the objective atonement of Christ." Sin is of such a nature that its forgiveness involved that death of that man on that cross.

As I have already indicated, the classical controversy between Muslim and Christian is the controversy concerning the Saviorhood of Jesus. It is this controversy which the new morality makes quite irrelevant. Can I say that I would rather be a Muslim whose ethical system has a transcendental reference, than a Christian whose ethics has contemporary relevance, so called, but has been cut loose from any connection with Christ's act of atonement?

Let me approach this question also in another way. The general category which the Bible uses to speak of the judgment of God, as it is exercised in the midst of human life, is to refer to everything that is condemned as the "imagination of men's hearts" (see Rom. 1:21). The contrast made is not between good and evil, or right and wrong, or between one form of religion and another. It is a contrast between that which is decided by man and that which is decided by God. The prohibition that man may not eat of the tree of the knowledge of good and evil is maintained (Gen. 2:17). In other words, the judgment of God with which men must live is this: that he does not allow men to usurp that which belongs to him alone. Some seek to fashion God in an image they like, so that they can have a god whom they can manipulate (Exod. 32:23); others seek to earn their salvation by works of merit, so that they can have a god whom they can anticipate (Matt. 7:21-23); still others seek themselves to execute God's judgment on their fellows, believing that they can have a god whom they can represent (Rom. 12:19). But God remains God and will not allow that in any way men take his place. He does scatter the proud in the imagination of their hearts (Luke 1:51).

We mistake the transcendental reference in ethical discussion when we think of it in terms of moral absolutes as such. The reference rather is simply and directly to God's Godhead. The Muslim defense of this transcendence is uncompromising. The Christian cannot be less so; for to compromise here will make meaningless the Christian insistence that he, of whom we speak, is Jesus, for he will save his people from their sins (Matt. 1:21).

Hinduism

The word for "Christians" in our part of the world is "Vedakarar." It means "the people of the Scriptures." That is the name which has been given to us by the Hindus. The Hindus have four Vedas—their scriptures; but we Christians are the people whom they call Vedakarar. How close this anomaly is to that earlier anomaly when the Jews called the Christians "the people of the Way." It is an anomaly symbolic of the relation in which Christianity is seen as standing toward Hinduism. Somehow, the claim that Jesus is the Christ of the Scriptures is recognized as a claim that Hinduism too has to reckon with in respect of its own scriptures. But no sooner do men seek to fit Jesus into the Hindu religious experience and teaching than he is seen as a contradiction of the central conviction for which Hinduism stands. Hinduism teaches that each man's religion is somewhere on the ladder of religious truth, and that no religion is false except when it claims to be the only and final truth. There is a contradiction between the kind of fulfillment which Jesus brings to man's religious quest and all the answers provided by the religions. It is with this contradiction between Jesus and religion that the Christian and the Hindu have to wrestle in their conversation with one another. The "religious man" can gladly accept the teachings of Jesus until the question is put: "Who do you say that I am?" But once the question is put, the "religious man" has only one answer, and that is to dismiss the question as pure foolishness. Indeed, it is as foolishness that this question of Jesus sounds in front of every Hindu temple.

I want to give here three illustrations of how the encounter between the Christian and the Hindu faiths looks in specific situations. Two people came to me asking me to solemnize their marriage. The girl was a Hindu convert to Christianity and the boy was a Hindu relative of hers. They came to me because the girl was insisting on a Christian marriage. The boy said to me, "I have no objection to a Christian marriage because, as a Hindu, I believe that it is the same God whom we all worship. You have your way of worshiping him and we have ours." My answer to him was that the difference did not lie in the different ways of worshiping the same God. "The Hindus," I said, "choose different stations of meeting where they can meet God, whereas Christians are bound by the faith that God has come to meet man in Jesus Christ. God himself has set up a station of meeting."

I take my second example from the Bible itself. It illustrates the form in which the ethical demand of the Christian faith cuts across the natural and normal ways in which a religious man would look at an ethical decision. Both the stories I shall refer to are about King Saul and the prophet Samuel. In the story of the king at Gilgal, Saul decided that the time had come to offer the sacrifice and, therefore, offered it himself because Samuel was late in coming (I Sam. 13:8-15). In the story of Saul and the Amalekites, Saul decided that it was better to offer the captured cattle as a sacrifice to God than to destroy them as Samuel had commanded (I Sam. 15:1-23). In both instances, there was no doubt about Saul's intentions. He wanted to do the religiously right thing. But, in both instances, the issue as Samuel posed it was, "Did you do the specific thing which the Lord commanded?"

The Christian faith is concerned constantly to testify to God's method of meeting man by specific revelation and command. It is this method of God which, the writer to the Hebrews claims, came to its culmination in Jesus Christ. In him the particulars culminated in the particular. God, who in many and various ways had spoken by the prophets, had now spoken by a Son whom he had appointed the heir of all things (Heb. 1:1-2)—so that it was with the heir that men had now to come to terms. To use another figure, in Jesus Christ the light of the world had become a lamp in a house. It had been put into men's hands, to be placed by them where they can walk by its light, or to be hid by them where they hope it will not disturb their darkness (John 1:9; Mark 4:21).

As a third illustration, I want to use a discussion going on in India today on the way in which, in thought and in practice, two movements are to be related. There is the movement by which it is sought to bring the treasures of Hinduism into the service of Christ, and there is the other movement which is concerned with taking Christ into the Hindu community but without raising with them the question of becoming Christians. Cannot we, it is asked, trust Jesus to make a place for himself within the Hindu religion and culture which is at the same time consonant with his identity as the Christ of God? In this discussion in India, there are protagonists on each side who would like to deny the legitimacy of the point of view and concern of the other. But, however difficult it may be to hold these two sides together, they surely belong together and, between them, provide the answer to the question of who he is.

This encounter between the Christian faith and the religious attitude as exemplified by Hinduism has also, in current theological debate, another thrust to it. Religion and the religious attitude are not only being challenged by the nature of the Christian faith, but they are also being challenged by what has come to be called the secular reformation. For a religious man, this life is a shadow of another realm of reality. Primitive examples will be: when a man thinks of a house, no more as a house, but as a home of ghosts; or of a tree, no more as a tree, but as the abode of spirits; or of an illness as the direct result of divine anger. The secularist will say that the religious man refuses to live life directly. The secularist is impatient with the religious attitude which is constantly seeking to relate the details of this secular life to another world. He is contemptuous of what he calls belief in a God out there or in a God of the gaps or in a God who is the reality behind the phenomena. If this is what it means to be religious, he would claim, the less religion the better.

This challenge to religion can also go one step further by the answer which it suggests—for instance, by one of the dominant answers suggested, which is to deny that God is a substantive reality at all. In the classical exposition of Hindu monism by Sankara, the position taken is that there is only one reality which is God. Man and human existence are adjectival to God. There are those today who, in the contemporary theological scene, have reversed this position. God is for them simply the right word to use when describing certain dimensions of human experience. God has become adjectival to man.

In this total discussion, it is easier to pick one's way if one is prepared to use the Jesus of history purely as a point of reference for experiences and ideas. The Hindu structure is fully hospitable to any type of religious experience, any system of religious or moral values, and any formulation of philosophical or theological ideas. Difficulties arise only when Jesus Christ, as a person, is thrust into the foreground and the question about his identity is raised. But should it prove true that it is illegitimate to ask that men should make up their minds about Jesus Christ himself, the actual person the

Gospels talk about, then it is much better and more satisfying to be a Hindu.

Communism

Buddhism, Islam, Hinduism—they represent the settled ways of our people. They are the "past" which an infant church confronts as it seeks to make Christ known and loved and obeyed. But there is also a "future" which is claiming adherents in our lands. The message of Communism has fallen on many receptive ears; for where men have for so long been content to let the ages slip by, the promise of Communism is indeed attractive. It promises that the future shall belong to man, the common man, and that the way to that future is in the Communist movement.

To whom does the future belong? The Christian is sure that it belongs to Christ. There is only one future tense in the church's creed: "He shall come again with glory to judge both the quick and the dead; whose kingdom shall have no end." Jesus is Lord—he is the Lord of the nations, he is above every principality and power, and the future belongs to him. He is not just One around whom people gather, seeking the solaces of private religion in a world of injustice and wrong; rather, he is the Lord of Hosts engaged in war with every form of evil, and under whose command men fight and inherit the kingdom that is to be. Pilate said to Jesus, "Do you not know that I have power to release you, and power to crucify you?" Jesus answered him, "You would have no power over me unless it had been given you from above" (John 19: 10-11). Pilate had power to crucify Jesus, but he had no power to stop the resurrection. The church may seem a weak and unimportant community when viewed against the march of Communism; but it keeps on getting in the way and repeating with maddening persistence the question of Jesus, "Who do men say that I am?" The question is a stumbling stone in front of every Communist procession.

The very fact that we can speak of Christianity in this way in relation to Communism shows that Christianity itself is a secular movement concerned with this world and with man's well-being in it. It is this secularity which is also responsible for the organizational structures of the Christian community. There is a form in which the Christian community exists in the world. This form has social, political, and even economic substance. If only the Communist movement can succeed in making Christianity function purely as a religion, it would then have no cause for fear. The point I am making is not that it is not possible for the Christian church to exist in a Communist country, for it is possible; but that wherever the church exists, it will exist in the form not only of a religious society, but of a secular movement. Both in the so-called Communist countries and the so-called democracies, the Christian church has to face the pressure to give up its claim that Jesus Christ is contemporary Lord of the life of the world and the peoples within it. However, there is no way of saying that Jesus is the Christ of God without resisting this pressure. Communist leaders are perceptive enough to see this secular quality of the Christian faith, and realistic enough to take it seriously.

But, it can be asked, is this secular sovereignty of Christ actually effective? I do not have the historical knowledge to give a substantial answer to this question, but I do know one thing which my faith teaches me. I know that the way God handles time is not man's way. He seems to take a thousand years to do what we would like him to do in a moment, and he does in a moment what we think cannot be done at all. The history of man viewed in the long stretches shows that the last word has never been with men and their best-laid plans, nor with armies and their most successful campaigns. The words of Jesus have constantly been proved to be true. "Every plant which my heavenly Father has not planted will be rooted up." (Matt. 15:13.)

Let me, in conclusion, link what I have sought to say in the above four areas of debate and dialogue with the central questions as we have seen them appear in the Gospel story. To recall these would reinforce my argument.

The Jew could not accept Jesus as the Son of man, for the Son of man he expected would come riding on the clouds of heaven, enthroned above life. Jesus came as suffering servant. Whether we talk of Buddhism, or any other form of humanism, the question to be decided is whether it is man who occupies the center of life's picture and, if so, which man?

Not only could the Jew not accept Jesus as the Son of man, he also could not accept him as the Son of God. He was expecting a deed of God to set men free from their ills. He did not have the slightest anticipation that God himself would come and live the human life. He had forgotten the full possibility of Emmanuel—"God with us." Whether we talk of Islam or any other religion which seeks to define the

127

divine absolute as inaccessible to human apprehension, the problem is, how is the "transcendent" related to the "here" and "now"? Is it only related as the over-against? What are the signs of the divine mercy?

The third controversy in which the Jew found himself involved, in dealing with Jesus Christ, was that he found it impossible to accept Jesus as the Christ of the Scriptures. Nothing is harder than to let the Lord himself make plain the meaning of the Scriptures that he has given. He came to his own home, says the Fourth Evangelist, and his own people would not receive him. They did not receive him because they were his own. They treated God's gifts as though these gifts were their own possession. His light had become their enlightenment; his truth had become their tradition; his words had become their Scriptures; and they would not take any risk with all these gifts which they believed God had entrusted to them. One of the most difficult problems for Hindus, indeed for all religious men whatever their religion, is to recognize and accept the ways in which God, who makes himself available to man, nevertheless maintains his freedom from the religious formulations, practices, and organizations which are the result of his own self-giving.

And lastly, faced by the proposition that Jesus Christ is Lord of the nations, he in whom the kingdom of God had come and would be consummated, the Jew could hardly believe it. Indeed, it was beyond belief. It did not fit any of the facts as he saw them. The situation is not very different today. As one looks at the world scene and assesses the contemporary strengths and weaknesses of the various movements of our time, the ideologies—whether Communist or non-Communist

—to which men have committed their allegiance, it seems futile to take seriously the words of Jesus, "Fear not, little flock, for it is your Father's good pleasure to give you the kingdom" (Luke 12:32).

So in our contemporary world and amidst its challenges men are asked to answer his question: "Who do you say that I am?" It is a question to be answered by a life of loyalty to him, and not in word only. To us, who already believe in him, and who, therefore, are committed also to press the question with others, the assurance given is this: that he himself will kindle the faith which will find the answer and supply the grace to live the answer out.

CHAPTER 6

The issue concerning who Jesus is, is more than an issue about his identity; it is also an issue about the ways of his Lordship, the way in which he maintains his "finality" in the life of the world and in his encounter with persons. These ways constitute the inner core of the experience of those who seek to witness to him and work for him. Indeed, since at the heart of the Christian witness lies the necessity both to talk about him and to point to him, there is, in the experience of those who have sought to commend him to others, an understanding of who he is which also demands as clear a statement as is possible. It is such a statement which we now attempt.

The word "mysteries" in the title "The Mysteries of the Kingdom" simply bears witness to the fact that, when we try to put into words the experience of the presence and Lordship of Jesus in the life and work of his witnesses, we find ourselves unable to do so except as a description of an experience which has in it the quality of participation in a mystery.

"The odyssey of the Spirit is eternal," writes Ernest Gordon, at the conclusion of his story, *Through the Valley of the Kwai.* "There are many resting places but no terminals. That is why the Letter to the Hebrews says, 'For here we have no continuing city, but seek one to come.'" Yes, for the mystery will remain until we see him face to face who alone is our final and permanent abode.

THE
MYSTERIES
OF
THE KINGDOM

As we live with Jesus and seek to serve him, we learn of him. What do we learn? What light does the experience of Christian work and witness throw on him on whom the work depends and about whom that witness is given? No answer to the question as to who Jesus is can be complete which does not include also the evidence of his witnesses.

The great commission, as found in Matthew's Gospel, is the natural text with which to begin a consideration of the experience of Christian witness. New Testament scholars tell us that the form of this text is the result of welding the words of Jesus in which he issued the commission with the experi-

131

ence of the disciples as they sought to carry it out. How does the great commission run? "All authority in heaven and on earth has been given to me. Go therefore and make disciples, baptize, and teach. Lo, I am with you always, to the close of the age." (See Matt. 28:18-20.) The command to go and to do is set within the context of a declaration and a promise. The disciples are told that, wherever they go and to whomsoever they go, there Jesus was already Lord. They would go representing his authority. And, precisely because he was Lord, Lord already, they would not go alone nor would they ever be left alone.

The disciples would go to do what? They would go to disciple the nations. Their task would be to make his sovereignty known and effective in the various forms of human community within which men lived. But there was also a second part to the commission. It was that they were to bring into one community, across the many boundaries that divide human communities, all those who acknowledge him. And both these things were to be done knowing that, wherever the disciples went and whatever they did, the Lord would be there with them and with those to whom they went in his name.

The church's work and witness is bounded by his authority and the ways in which he will exercise it, as well as by the promise of his presence and the ways in which he will be there. To put it in another way, the great commission does not spell out a task to be performed, a work to be done, the ways of doing which can be devised by those who do it; nor is the promise, "I am with you always," simply a promise of supporting grace and empowering companionship. Rather, the authority would continue to remain his, and he would be there wherever his disciples went, so that whatever they did and how they did it would be subject constantly both to the affirmation and negation of what he himself would be doing and how he was doing it.

In this experience, the mystery is the result of the fact that we never do know fully in what manner he is where he is, or how he is doing what he is doing. We know so little of the forms in which he exercises his Lordship or the immediate ends toward which, in any particular situation, he is working. Indeed, the promise, "I am with you always and everywhere, and I shall be with you to the end," is not altogether a comfort. We know only too well that it is his presence with us which is the basic cause of many of our problems.

No one who has taken part in any contemporary discussion of the missionary enterprise of the church, whether in its classical form as missions or according to its most inclusive definition as mission, can be unaware of the fact that the church has been overtaken by a crisis in understanding of what the mission of the church really is and how it is to be fulfilled. This crisis in understanding is the result of many factors, but primarily it stems from a fresh awareness of the ways in which the mission of the church is involved in the mysteries of the kingdom. What we do as his disciples is conditioned so constantly by who he is and the ways in which he maintains his identity.

These mysteries I would enumerate as the mystery of his presence, the mystery of his demand, the mystery of his purpose, the mystery of his tokens, and the mystery of his grace. We shall consider them one by one.

133

The Mystery of His Presence

The first part of the great commission is to disciple the nations. This is an impossible task, except as Jesus himself is present and actively at work within the various forms of human community. As is well known, the word "nation" in the Bible does not refer to a nation-state in the modern sense of the word, but rather to any form of human association in which people together accept a common life.

This presence of Jesus within community life has, in large measure, to be a presence incognito. In the Old Testament, it is this presence which the prophets interpret when they assume that the one God whom Israel acknowledged and worshiped is the God of all the nations too. It is his rule which they declare to be effective in all the world. But not only is Christ thus present within the common forms of community life, he is present also in the life that people live within the various religions. In seeking to discern this presence, account must be taken of the fact that each man is both more than and less than the religion he professes. He is less than the religion he professes because he never lives up to its highest teachings in faith or morals. However, he is also more than the religion he professes because in every man's life there are those experiences and intuitions of God which transcend his religious profession. They constitute an overspill in his religious life. This overspill exists in the life of Christians also; for Christianity, as a religious system, is never adequate enough to include or express every aspect of a person's experience of the Triune God. In religious dialogue, it is when men speak out of this overspill that they really begin to speak helpfully to one another.

The basic question, in speaking of the presence of Christ incognito, is not whether we can always discern him when he is thus present, but whether it is part of his will that he should thus be present in community as well as in personal life. I can witness to the fact, and I am sure many others can, of the perception of his presence among persons and situations where he was neither known nor acknowledged. Indeed, the clear teaching of Jesus was that this would be so. Not only did he imply this in all that he said concerning the nature of God's kingdom and his own Lordship, but he also made it explicit in such a parable as that of the sheep and the goats, in which the central issue turns on his presence in anonymity.

Side by side with the commission to disciple the nations goes the command to baptize those who believe. In the Christian community, thus constituted, is the sacrament of his known presence—his presence in the breaking of bread, his presence where two or three are gathered in his name, his presence where his disciples go in mission, his presence where the gospel is proclaimed. This complex life of the Christian community, composed of persons from every nation, is the basis of the reply that always must be given when the response of someone to the impact of the gospel is: What must I do? Peter said on the day of Pentecost, "Repent and be baptized." Paul gave the same reply to the jailer at Philippi (Acts 2:38; 16:33).

The two parts of the great commission, then, belong together and, in their relation to each other, lead those who

135

undertake them into the experience of the mystery of Christ's presence. For the mystery lies here: that we can never be sure where he is content to be incognito and where he demands to be acknowledged; nor are we certain of what the specific form is of the acknowledgment which, in any particular situation, he demands.

I had the privilege of discussing this question with Bishop R. O. Hall of Hong Kong, whose point of view I found most stimulating because of his long experience as a missionary among Chinese people. When I raised with him this problem of the relation between the presence of the Christ incognito and the task of gathering together as a visible community those who acknowledge Christ, he replied: "This perhaps is where in China and among Chinese people our concern is a little different, perhaps because Chinese people have no community religions. 'Being Chinese' is the basic religion of Chinese people. They have no sense of a bond based on faith or religion, nor, I think, should Christianity in its truest sense limit itself to a Christian community. I think Christ's biggest break with Judaism was replacing community religion by the revelation of an existing, ever-present, everywhere rule of God over all men and all history. But your duty and your joy, like mine, is—in prayer and life and love, in deed and word and thought—to be intent on this one thing: that the light of the knowledge of the glory of God in the face of Jesus Christ should be known and accepted in every human heart."

Reading the letter from Bishop Hall, I found myself saying, "Yes, I agree"; but the consequence of the mystery still remains. For what does it mean to have the light of the knowledge of the glory of God in the face of Jesus Christ known and accepted in every human heart? What is the connection between acceptance and acknowledgment? Are there those who have accepted Jesus in the form or forms in which he has come to them, but who nevertheless have not acknowledged him because they do not know that it is he whom they have accepted? And can we, on the basis of this possibility, treat the open acknowledgment of Jesus, as Lord and Savior, as an extra about which there need be no concern? And yet, precisely where there is that concern, is not the warning of Bishop Hall right—that any answer which makes the need to become a member of the Christian community a reason for turning Christianity into a community religion is a false answer?

In spite of our inability, then, to probe the mystery of his presence, can we still set out for ourselves what the consequence may be of this mystery for the Christian mission? I think we can, and that we can formulate this consequence in terms of three obligations. There is, first of all, the obligation to spread Christian influence and to distribute the Christian presence in such a way as to help acceptance of Jesus and his will even where he is present incognito. How often have we heard people, who are not themselves Christians, say in some particular situation, "Let us do the Christian thing, for that is the only right thing to do." To make this kind of reaction more and more possible must increasingly determine the strategy of the Christian mission. Secondly, there is the obligation to discern and identify Christ's presence, as far as we are able to do it, wherever that presence is, so that with increasing sureness we may be able to point to him in such a way that others may see. This obligation to discern and identify can never be fulfilled except as those who are engaged in the Christian mission learn to listen to what is actually being said by those of beliefs other than Christian, by the other religions themselves, and by the cultures which are the fruits of these religions. Often we are so concerned to tell the good news that we miss hearing it. And, thirdly, there is the obligation, as opportunity arises, to press the question: Will you follow him, will you acknowledge him, will you become his disciple, will you join the company of those who not only believe but also are seeking to elicit faith? The issue is whether in a world where there are so many names that people can bear and by which they can be identified, one is prepared to bear Christ's name and to be known among others as one of his men. Of course the problem remains as to how to engage in this kind of questioning of others without violating their personalities. The dividing line between persuasion and propaganda is a very difficult line to keep.

The Mystery of His Demand

The first mystery, the mystery of his presence, which raises the question of what he will have us do, is set within a second mystery, the mystery of what he himself is doing. The decisive question has to be not whether we think that people ought to become Christians, but whether he thinks so.

When we read the Gospels we find that Jesus dealt with people in different ways. His common attitude to those who came to him and sought his help was simply to give them the help they asked for. Bartimaeus received his sight, the leper was cleansed, the daughter of Jairus was raised from the dead, the epileptic boy was healed, the paralytic was forgiven—but in none of these cases did Jesus follow up what he did for them with any request that they become his disciples. In the sermon which he preached at Nazareth, he quoted the words of the prophet: "God has sent me to release the captive, to give sight to the blind, to set free the oppressed, to bring good news to the poor" (see Luke 4:18-19)—and, throughout his ministry, he treated these as ends in themselves. To use a term that has been common in discussion for many years, Jesus seems never to have been a believer in indirect evangelism. In fact, his practice makes any talk of indirect evangelism sound quite stupid. The mercies of God to men and women in their several needs are mercies pure and simple.

However, this was not his only way with people. When the woman with a hemorrhage wanted to remain anonymous, he would not allow her to do so. He identified her and made her meet him in person. After the blind man who washed himself in the pool of Siloam was cured, Jesus met him and asked him, "Do you believe in the Son of man?" He then revealed his identity to the man, eliciting faith. In the case of the man who had been ill for thirty-eight years, who was cured at the pool of Bethzatha, Jesus met him again and admonished him to sin no more. In these examples, and others like them, we see how Jesus went beyond the actual deed of kindness performed to effect a personal meeting between himself and those whom he had helped.

Yet again, how different this way of his was from his way with Peter and Andrew, James and John, Matthew, and the rich young man! In each of these cases, the demand he made had the force of a command: "Leave your nets"; "Leave your parents"; "Leave your employment"; "Sell what you have." In the parable of the wedding feast, when the master sent out his servants to bring guests from the highways and by-ways, his word to the servants was, "Go, and compel them to come in" (see Luke 14:23). There were those in the ministry of Jesus who felt this compulsion.

Nevertheless, not merely was the rich man permitted freely to reject the demand of Christ, there were also those others whose request that they follow him, he himself rejected. The man at Gadara is a case in point. The story tells us how Jesus wrestled with this man in conversation, seeking to find him and to find for him his lost self. When the man finally came to his right mind, he made one request: "I want to go with you." But Jesus asked him to go home instead, and to his responsibilities there; and there, where God had placed him, to speak of what God had done for him (Luke 8:26-39). Again, when the ten lepers were cured, and the one Samaritan came back to give God thanks, Jesus was satisfied to leave it there. He asked for no expression of gratitude to himself (Luke 17:11-19). He was content when, as a result of his ministry, men found in God the one whom they must glorify and the one to whom they must be grateful.

In addition to these incidents illustrating his different ways with men, account must be taken also of the incident of the three men who met with him on his way to Jerusalem. To the first who wanted to follow him, he presented his demand in such a way that the man withdrew; and yet we know how, across the centuries, Jesus has accepted the discipleship of countless men and women whose motives have been equally

mixed, and whose initial dedication was, at its best, very in-
complete. The second man involved in this incident wanted
some adjustment between his obligations at home and his
service of Jesus. Jesus refused to make any such adjustments.
But how patient Jesus has been with so many since, allowing
them to find their answer to the total demands of his service.
The third man in the story was a man whom Jesus himself
called. The man was willing, but was not ready to start immediately. Jesus refused to wait for him. And yet, with what
understanding has he waited for so many of his followers
who, if not for that waiting, would not have become members
of his company.

Is it not obvious, then, that as we review these many and
different ways of Jesus with people, we find ourselves at the
heart of a mystery? The issue again is not what it is that we
must do as we go to men in his name, but what it is that we
find him doing and what his demands for them are. Some
consequences of this mystery for our discipleship, however,
are clear. It is clear, first of all, that it is never permissible to
use the meeting of human need as an occasion for pressing
the claims of Christ for discipleship; neither is there any reason why the work of meeting human need should not be done
together by those who bear his name and those who do not.
Here is a common area where those who acknowledge him
and those who serve him in his incognito can work together.
It is clear also that if the commission is a double one—to
disciple the nations as well as to baptize disciples—we should
be willing to allow even some of those who are prepared to
acknowledge Christ to take him into their own cultures and
perhaps even into their own religions. One of the difficult

problems which has become theologically acute today is how to define this penumbra of the Christian community. This problem is all the more urgent because everywhere the Christian community, being in numbers a minority community, is constantly tempted by this minority position to become a communal group. How Christians may be not a communality but a true community, in responsive and responsible relation to other human communities and to the human community as a whole, has become an insistent question. However, having raised these questions, let it still be quite clear that none of them are truly faced unless they are faced in relation to the unchanging demand of the gospel that it be proclaimed in season and out of season, and that the acceptance of it be always pressed with urgency. When the Word is proclaimed and the demand for discipleship is made explicit, there can be no blurring of the issues involved.

At this point I want to quote a letter telling a story which, it seems to me, has quite a direct reference to what we have been considering. The story is of an incident in Ceylon which, when I heard it from the Rev. Basil Jackson, I asked him to put in letter form, so that I may quote it. Mr. Jackson is a Methodist missionary in Ceylon. This is what he wrote:

My dear Daniel,

Here is the letter you wanted. Many years ago I used to visit a very remote Buddhist village, Laggala, with a group of students who were training to be evangelists. We tried to be the "Christian Presence" in that village. We took simple medicines with us, and each morning we held a simple "dispensary." There was a young man who came, morning after morning, wanting help. He had deep festering sores all round his shoulder and armpit. The

142

local apothecary confirmed our suspicion that he was suffering from a deep-seated tubercular affection of the glands. There was nothing we could do. Our simple remedies would be quite useless. However, it was impossible to take him all the way to the Kandy hospital. It was too far, too remote, and too foreign. He would have died of fright and loneliness.

On the last day, I explained all this to the boy's father, and offered to have a service of prayer in his house. The father gladly agreed. There was a big crowd present in the house and courtyard. We had a simple service, including the reading of the story of the healing of the paralytic, prayer, and laying on of hands. At the end of the service, the father stood up before his neighbors and declared, "If the boy gets well, I will be baptized." Next morning we came away. For many weeks we had no news. There was no post available in those days. But we remembered the boy regularly in our intercession groups.

Some four months later, we returned to Laggala. We found the young man completely cured. My first instinct was to go and remind the father of his promise; but something held me back. I was reluctant to do it, although my companions urged me to do so. I met the father, but we talked of other things. I made no reference to his declaration to be baptized. I myself was puzzled to know why I had felt led to remain silent. But thinking about it afterward, I realized that that was what Jesus himself did. He never followed up his healing with any demand of discipleship. He was concerned to bring healing; his making of disciples seemed always to have been quite a different and unconnected operation.

Moreover, I did not want to appear to the people of Laggala as broker, arranging transactions between them and God—"If God does this or that, then I will become his follower"—that would be to build up a completely false idea of God in their minds. Nor did I want to show forth God as a sort of miracle man or wonder-worker. To have used this healing as a springboard for presenting the gospel might well have gained a substantial number of converts, but they would be disciples for the wrong reasons, and they would have a faith in a God quite different from him who was revealed in Christ. There are practically no Christians in Laggala today. I have often felt thankful that I did not help to create a group of spurious Christians.

Yours,
Basil

The Mystery of His Purpose

How clearly the two mysteries, that of his presence and that of his demand, together point to a third mystery, that of his purpose. Paul, in his letter to the Ephesians, speaks of the way in which the richness of God's free grace has been lavished upon those who have become his sons through Jesus Christ. Not only have they received, he says, their share in the heritage which is the result of God's design whose purpose is everywhere at work, but they have also been imparted insight into this design and purpose, which is that the universe, all in heaven and on earth, might be brought into a unity in Christ (Eph. 1:9-14). God is working at two things. On the one hand, there is his inclusive purpose to bring all into a unity in Christ; and, on the other hand, there is his exclusive purpose to create a community who will be the demonstration of this unity and evidence of Christ's reconciling power. In the working out of these two purposes, what God does with respect to each serves to further the other. The mystery lies in this overlap.

What are the implications of this overlap? The first thing to say is that we are always involved in the carrying out of the exclusive purpose of God, of which we ourselves are part of the result. The building up of the church is an on-going responsibility; so that it is a matter of great concern when the church in any particular place does not grow in numbers. The mysteries that we have been speaking about must never serve to dull the ardor of the church to spread the gospel and to have men and women openly accept Jesus Christ as Lord and Savior. Often the problem is that we either tend to find in these mysteries a sufficient salve for our disturbed consciences when the church does not grow, or we tend to forget the mysteries and simply get down to working out better methods of evangelism and better strategies for mission. There is no simple way of living with a mystery, and all the more so when the mystery is a mystery of God. But essential to Christian obedience will always be this matter of living with his mysteries, of accepting responsibility without impinging on his sovereignty, of learning to hope in him without making that hope an escape from actuality, of working as if everything depended on how we work without forgetting that it is by his work that the building is built.

In connection with the inescapable responsibilities involved in the building up of the church, it is important not to pass in silence one possible confusion. There is all the world of difference between the building up of the church and the maintenance of a particular form of church life and organization. Let me give an example that lies closest to my own situation. As I write this, my church in Ceylon is facing a financial crisis. Seven years ago we became financially independent of mission aid to maintain the basic structure which we had inherited from our missionary forebears. We have now reached the point of recognizing that the structure we have inherited has little relation to our financial resources. What do we do? There is a tendency to say, Let us go back to missionary aid. There is also the wisdom which says, You are not building up a church as long as it does not rest on a local foundation. A prefabricated building may not need a foundation, but it cannot be called a church.

This example is not a digression. We must realize that if the building up of the church and the creation of the unity of all things in Christ belong together, then the forms in which the church is built up must be congruent with the larger purposes within which it is set. To put the matter simply, the life of any church must represent the actual life that the members of that church live in their particular world, which will always have its own culture, its own forms of religious plurality, its own interdependent social structures, and its own financial base. Only so can the church bring to the service of the kingdom the "all things" that are to be reconstituted in Christ.

Indeed, the implication of God's double purpose goes even beyond this. For, if the inclusive purpose of God is this purpose of reconciliation by which unity is created of all things, then the reconciling power of Christ must be the chief characteristic of the life of the church. The Christian community is a community of forgiven people who have learned to live with one another as those who can forgive and be forgiven and who, therefore, are both the instruments and the demonstration of Christ's work of reconciliation. The experience of the forgiveness of sins and the taking away of the sense of guilt are experiences which are common to all religions. Whether a religion testifies to an experience of forgiveness which is the result of God's grace, or to an experience of forgiveness which is the result of each person expiating his own sin, or to an experience of forgiveness which is the result of counterbalancing evil deeds by good deeds, the experience of forgiveness testified to is a real one. The peculiarity of the forgiveness that one experiences in Christ is that it necessarily issues in one's participation in Christ's forgiving and reconciling ministry. There is only one forgiveness, his forgiveness of all men, so that to forgive and to be forgiven belong together in an inescapable connection. The implications of this connection become startlingly clear when one considers the fact of a divided church. For if the reconciling power of Jesus Christ is found not to be enriched by these differences, it is because a divided church has construed the mystery of God's double purpose to its own advantage. It has cut adrift his purpose in calling the church into being from his purpose to reconstitute all things in unity in Christ.

The Mystery of His Tokens

The fourth and fifth mysteries belong together and are concerned with the ways of God with each person. When one comes to his first conscious experience of the mercy of God in Christ, one is constantly surprised by the ways in which prayers are answered and his presence is assured. I have often explained progress in the Christian life, both to myself and to other people, by comparing it to the way in which parents deal with their children. When children are small, more often than not parents give them the little things they ask for: a new dress, a doll, some chocolates, bat and ball, and so on. Parents know when a child is too small to understand a refusal. But as the child grows, he begins to find that the number of times father or mother says "No" is increasing. This process goes on until growing understanding between child and parents makes it unnecessary to say "No" very often. The way in which God deals with us has seemed to me like this. As one matures in the Christian life, one begins to recognize that in large measure one has to live without interference from him in the kind of causal universe to which our world belongs. If I fall from a window of an apartment house, no amount of prayer can stop my going down. It may be that my clothes may get caught on some protuberance and my fall be arrested; but that kind of thing will be rare. If I should get measles or chicken pox, no amount of praying will reduce the days of quarantine. Should a country be poor and there be want of food, prayer for oneself or one's family cannot by itself avail. Food is necessary for the whole community, if it is to be provided for any member of it. This is the kind of world in which we live. And yet, we do get from God, from time to time, personal tokens of his mercy and his presence. Accidents happen, but sometimes there is unexpected safety provided. Sickness comes, but there is given through it some experience which brings the assurance that God is there. It is this assurance that we lose when, in experiences such as these, we say: That prayer was answered because it was according to God's will and this prayer was not answered because it was not according to God's will. For the point of the token is that it is intended to tell us that God is there, both when we get tokens and when we do not.

This experience is all the more true in our work for him. Now and again, and only now and again, we get tokens of the ways in which our work is blessed. Someone tells us that he was helped by a prayer we prayed; or another tells us of help received through a sermon or a book; or in some committee we are led to say something which helps to make decision easier. However, these are only tokens. Countless days pass without any token whatever. And yet one knows, by the tokens that one has already received, that God is always there, that his mercy is forever sure and that his steadfast love never fails.

Why does God deal with us like this? Many helpful things can be said in answer to this question. But ultimately the mystery still remains. So that there is no other affirmation that faith can make except to say that no experience can nullify the message the tokens bring. In this assertion of God's love, Paul does not rule out the possibility of any of life's difficult experiences. Neither death nor life, he says, nor the assault of powers beyond the powers of men, nor any experience whether in the present or in the future, nor any achievement, nor ambition, nor frustration, nor despair, can separate us from the love of God in Christ Jesus, our Lord (Rom. 8:38-39).

Concurrently with writing this, I was reading the book by Ernest Gordon entitled *Through the Valley of the Kwai*. The whole thrust of the book is to show how the tokens of God's mercy and presence were given to men, some of whom were believers in Christ and others not, under circumstances where the overall situation said, if it said anything at all, that if there was a God, he was a God who did not care. The miracle which the book talks about is the miracle of how men learned to cling to these tokens and to live by them; and the miracle of how, again and again, the tokens given were given through people. It was men who exemplified God's love, God's self-giving, God's patience, and the hope that has its origin only in God.

One incident in the book turned my mind also to another aspect of this way of God with men. It is an incident concerning a man called Dusty, an orderly, about whom Gordon tried to get news after their release from prison. This is how Gordon relates the story.

At last I met a [prisoner] who had been on the same work detail with him.

"Yes, I knew him," he said. "We were sent to Burma to cut a retreat route for the Japs. He was one of those left behind after the road was built to maintain it during the monsoon."

"Where is he now?" I asked.

The man was reluctant to speak. He stammered for a minute or two. Then he replied,

"We had a pretty bad time of it. It was a repeat performance of the railroad. And those who were left behind had an even harder time—especially after the Japs knew they were going to lose."

He stopped.

"But what about Miller?" I asked again.

The man looked away.

"The last news I had of him wasn't good."

"What was it then?"

"According to what I heard, he was in trouble."

"Dusty?"

"He got the Nip warrant officer in charge of his party down on him."

"What had he done wrong?"

"That was it. He hadn't done anything wrong." He swallowed hard. "The Nip hated him because he couldn't break him. You know how he was—a good man if ever there was one. That's why he hated him."

"What did the Nip do to him?"

"He strung him up to a tree."

I was aghast.

"You mean—"

Then came the simple reply,

"Yes. He crucified him."

I could hardly speak.

"When?"

"About the beginning of August."

"Just before the Japs—"

"—packed up, yes."

He turned away. He had said as much as he could bear.

I was so stunned I didn't quite know what to do. I walked out from the group of chattering questioners.

Dusty dead?

Dusty—the man of deep faith and the warm heart—the man who was incapable of a mean act, even against a brutal tormentor. He had been rewarded for his goodness by hatred—his radiant goodness which must have maddened the warrant officer to the point where he went berserk.

There, like his Master, he died, so far from his homeland, so far from everyone, yet so near to God.

I have quoted this story, because this is the first instance I have read in which goodness was crucified because it became unbearable. How near the token is to the meaning of Calvary. No study of the story of Jesus, as told in the Gospels, should ever be allowed to be independent of the repetition of that story in the lives of men all down the centuries. When various forms of New Testament criticism have got rid of this miracle or that, or cast doubt upon this incident or that, one suddenly finds oneself confronted by a repetition. For many of us, for instance, in our part of the world, the life of Sadhu Sundar Singh brought many of these tokens. The Sadhu was one of those who saw the risen Lord. Dusty's death and Sadhu Sundar Singh's experiences are part of God's provision for faith. So also are the experiences of countless people who testify that what Jesus is reported to have done by the Gospel writers, he has repeated in their own lives.

The mystery of it is: Why the token to him and not to me? Why a token in that situation and not in this? Why that kind of token there and this kind here? To these questions there is no answer. The mystery remains a mystery, but a mystery which both challenges faith and nourishes it.

The Mystery of His Grace

All this leads directly into the central mystery, which is the mystery of his grace. In its crudest form, the problem is stated in the question: If God's grace has found me, why not him? It is no answer to say that he has rejected God's grace, that he has no faith. For according to the teaching of the New Testament, faith also is a gift, and so is repentance.

It is by the Holy Spirit that we are taught to know God as Father—each one to know God as his Father. We simply get into trouble when we say that salvation is by grace, while at the same time affirming without reservation the free will of man. Whether we are saved or damned, the judgment pronounced is in Christ and by Christ and within the act of his atonement. Every person whom Christ judges is a person for whom he has died.

One direction, along which we find an attempt made in the New Testament to understand this mystery, is that of the doctrine of predestination. But the way in which this doctrine is often discussed makes the mystery of God's grace a mystery of darkness and not of light. I do not intend to discuss this doctrine here. All I intend, by mentioning it, is to point out how central the mystery is about which we are speaking. Charles Wesley expresses one side of this mystery in verses such as these:

> Thy undistinguishing regard
> Was cast on Adam's fallen race:
> For all Thou hast in Christ prepared
> Sufficient, sovereign, saving grace.

> The world he suffered to redeem;
> For all he hath the atonement made;
> For those that will not come to him
> The ransom of his life was paid.

But it is the same Charles Wesley who states the other side of the mystery:

> Sinners, turn: why will you die?
> God, your Savior, asks you why;

God, who did your souls retrieve,
Died himself, that you might live.
Will you let him die in vain?
Crucify your Lord again?
Why, you ransomed sinners, why
Will you slight his grace, and die?

There is no way of speaking both of God's sufficient, sovereign, saving grace, and of man's freedom to accept or reject it without getting involved in contradiction. But on that contradiction depends the seriousness of man's situation when he is presented with the gospel as well as the unconditional good news which the gospel represents. As we go to others with the message of Christ, we must learn to see them illumined by the gospel hope; whereas, whenever we look at ourselves, we must never forget the warning that we who have preached to others may ourselves be set aside (I Cor. 9:27).

It is not enough, however, to approach this mystery of God's grace from within a consideration of the difficulties implicit in our understanding of salvation and damnation. Some clue to this mystery must lie also in the fact that when we speak of God's grace, we are actually speaking of God's gracious presence itself in and with the world, as well as in and with the church. The Lord of the world is the head of the church, so that part of the mystery we are seeking to probe will be in the relation between the church and the world. There is a way of so misunderstanding this relation that the world is looked upon as a kind of ocean from which fish must be caught to be put inside a churchly aquarium. The truth lies rather in the opposite direction, for part of the mystery of grace is that God's gracious presence is fully operative in the world, even though it is by avowed response to this grace that the church is constituted.

Paul, writing to the Colossians, draws their attention to the fact that in Jesus, who is head of the body, the church, all things are held together, and through him God chose to reconcile the whole universe to himself—through him alone (Col. 1:18-20). If God's gracious presence is thus operative in the world, then the clue to the mystery of salvation and damnation cannot lie exclusively in the nature of men's response to grace, which is the constitutive factor in the life of the church. It must lie also in the nature of the response to grace which is part of the life of the world.

Speaking on this aspect of grace at the Free Church Federal Council of Great Britain recently, Dr. Norman Goodall, the moderator, said, "It is the business of Freed Churchmen (of whatever denomination)—of churchmen freed by grace—to go into all the world discerning the presence and ways of grace, learning what it means for men to be obedient to grace in the centers of the world's authorities and corridors of power, in the new world of technologists and the nuclear physicists, on the experimental frontiers of the arts, within the struggle to learn afresh what it means in human behavior to live by love and not by law. Here are the areas in which freed churchmen—not only Free Churchmen—may find one another and know God and learn those contemporary words which spring from the timeless Word."

The accent falls on going into all the world and discerning the presence and ways of grace. Since God is the mystery we have to live with, the way to live with him is to go with him wherever he goes and to be available to him for whatever he is working at. The mystery of God is not so much a mystery to be understood as to be encompassed by. We do not resolve it, we are upheld by it. He puts us to work, enabling us, by the work we do, to grapple with the consequences of the mystery, even though the mystery itself remains. We collect the straw, we bake the bricks, we mix the cement, but he is the builder. We do not do his work, we serve it.

And, what is he building? What is he doing? He is not building a church but a kingdom. He is not collecting Christians, he is redeeming creation. So will prayer concerning whatever is done in his name befit the confession made concerning him:

Lord, let thy servants see thee at thy saving work,
And let their children see thy glorious power.
May thy loving favor rest on us, prospering the work we undertake,
And when our work is done, establish thou it.

(See Psalm 90:16-17.)

WHO IS THIS JESUS?

D. T. Niles

With the simplicity of a direct conversation the author examines the Gospel stories of Jesus to see what he is like.

Yet this simplicity is deceiving. Here is profound Christology, sound biblical theology—an in-depth look at the biblical testimony to Jesus Christ that sets the evidence within the confusions and controversies of religious debate today.

In six chapters D. T. Niles examines the Gospels in detail to get at the story of what Jesus is like. He works from four basic questions. What does Jesus look like when we look at him? What does it feel like when he looks at us? What does it seem like when he is presented to others? What does he act like when we go with him on the way?

He is convinced that only as we listen to the biblical testimony in its actual language and idiom can we interpret the record for our day and our generation.

D. T. Niles sees a central, moving theme that runs throughout the Gospels as he presents his picture of Jesus in such a way that the reader will thrill to this intimate encounter with the Christ of experience.